Journey Through
Philippians

TARA BARNDT

Copyright © 2019 by Tara Barndt

All rights reserved. This book or any portion thereof may not be reproduced or used in any manner whatsoever without the express written permission of the publisher except for the use of brief quotations in a book review.

Printed in the United States of America

First Printing, 2019

Print ISBN: 978-1-54396-126-3

eBook ISBN: 978-1-54396-127-0

Dedication

To my husband, Jeremy.

Thank you for encouraging me to write this devotional and for believing God had given me something to share. Thank you for supporting me all through the writing process.

Thank you, Linda Craft, for bringing me along with you into leading and teaching women's Bible studies. I wouldn't have started without you.

Thank you, Katherine Hwang, Sarah Smith, Harriet Calcaterra, and Joel Fitzpatrick for your editing expertise and input.

Thank you to my parents who gave me encouragement and a love for reading and writing.

Thank you to my gracious heavenly Father who began and will complete His good work in me.

"Paul's letter to the Philippians spoke joy to his beloved friends, and in *Journey through Philippians* Tara Barndt guides us as a trusted and transparent friend through the riches of this epistle. She has studied the biblical text carefully, so her interpretation is reliable. More than that, the biblical text has searched her own heart, so her surrender to Christ's Spirit makes her application hit home. Best of all, *Journey through Philippians* returns, again and again, as the epistle does, to Christ himself, who defines our identity, sustains us in suffering, shows us servanthood, and graciously grants the righteousness that our best efforts could never achieve. Taking this journey will lead you to love, trust, and follow Jesus more joyfully."

> ~**DENNIS E. JOHNSON, Ph.D.**, Professor Emeritus of Practical Theology Westminster Seminary California and author of *Philippians* (Reformed Expository Commentary)

"Simple, practical and steeped in the gospel. In *Journey Through Philippians* by Tara Barndt you will be encouraged in the gospel and challenged in your walk with Christ. If you are looking for an accessible, section by section guide through the book of Philippians be sure to pick up this book."

> ~**JOEL FITZPATRICK**, Pastor, speaker and author of *Mom, Dad... What's Sex?*, *Between Us Guys* and contributor to *The Sinner/Saint Devotional*

CONTENTS

Introduction ~ Philippians 1:2 1
Day 1 ~ Philippians 1:1, 3-5, 7-8 5
Day 2 ~ Philippians 1:6 9
Day 3 ~ Philippians 1:9-11 13
Day 4 ~ Philippians 1:12-14 15
Day 5 ~ Philippians 1:15-18 19
Day 6 ~ Philippians 1:19-20 21
Day 7 ~ Philippians 1:21-26 23
Day 8 ~ Philippians 1:27-28 27
Day 9 ~ Philippians 1:29-30 31
Day 10 ~ Philippians 2:1-2 33
Day 11 ~ Philippians 2:3-4 37
Day 12 ~ Philippians 2:5-7 41
Day 13 ~ Philippians 2:8 45
Day 14 ~ Philippians 2:9-11 47
Day 15 ~ Philippians 2:12-13 49
Day 16 ~ Philippians 2:14-16 53
Day 17 ~ Philippians 2:17-18 55
Day 18 ~ Philippians 2:19-24 57
Day 19 ~ Philippians 2:25-30 61
Day 20 ~ Philippians 3:1-3 65
Day 21 ~ Philippians 3:4-6 67
Day 22 ~ Philippians 3:7-8 69
Day 23 ~ Philippians 3:9-11 71
Day 24 ~ Philippians 3:12-14 73
Day 25 ~ Philippians 3:15-16 77
Day 26 ~ Philippians 3:17-21 79
Day 27 ~ Philippians 4:1-5 83

Day 28 ~ Philippians 4:6-7 87
Day 29 ~ Philippians 4:8-9 91
Day 30 ~ Philippians 4:11-13 95
Day 31 ~ Philippians 4:10, 14-18 97
Day 32 ~ Philippians 4:19-20 101
Day 33 ~ Philippians 4:21-23 103
Songs for Philippians 105

*All Scripture references and quotes are taken from the ESV.

Introduction ~ Philippians 1:2

Grace to you and peace from God our Father and the Lord Jesus Christ.

For years, I have read through Paul's letters and quickly sailed over the "grace and peace" greetings. I know what grace and peace are after all, so let's get on to the real meat. Little did I know how much I was missing in those three words.

The Greek word for grace is *charis*. Grace is God's unmerited favor granted or gifted to sinful man. In Paul's greeting is a reminder of God's free gift of salvation, an exhortation to respond in thankfulness, and a prayer asking for God's abiding favor as we face daily needs and trials. We can do nothing apart from Him. What an encouragement it must have been to the Philippians to have Paul's reminder of God's grace in their salvation and sanctification. God had them covered.

There is another similar word used thirty-eight times in the New Testament. It is *eucharisteō*, a verb meaning "to be grateful or to give thanks." It contains the word *charis* (grace). Another word based on *charis* is *chara* meaning joy (Used five times in Philippians, and the verb "rejoice", *chairō*, is appears eleven times in Philippians.). Together, these three words give me a picture of a beautiful swirl of thankfulness and joy in light of God's gifts of grace, making this grace-greeting even richer.

The Greek word for *peace* is *eirene*. It is the peace or rest we have in the assurance of our salvation through Christ's atoning work alone. The Hebrew word *shalom* may be more familiar. As the Jewish people may have been in the habit of saying "shalom" like our "hi," we can gloss over Paul's greeting without a second thought, but his words are chock-full of meaning. To say "peace" to someone was to wish for them a foretaste of the Messianic age to come: to be complete and whole, to be healthy, to be safe, to be prosperous, to be tranquil, to be rested, to be happy, to be free from discord or agitation. When was the last time you prayed for a brother or sister in Christ to have a foretaste of heaven?

I know. That is an abundance of Greek and definitions that may still seem like they belong in a seminary and not in your everyday life. However, those words have begun to change the way I approach my day and how I pray for others. I am learning to meditate daily on just how amazing God's grace is. Sometimes I am vividly aware of my sinfulness. On those days I sink into God's grace. I am thankful for the blessing of His undeserved grace and mercy; that He is seeing me through Jesus' righteousness not covered in my own sin. Other days I miss that log in my eye, and I forget to show any acknowledgment or gratitude. Some days are even great. My sin seems limited to a stray thought. I've nailed righteous for a little while (probably missing a log again). But every day, good or bad, every hour, every minute, I need God's grace. All my righteousness is as filthy rags, and I am just as desperate for God and His grace in my good moments and as in my bad.

"The sinner does not need more grace than the saint, nor does the immature and undisciplined believer need more than the godly, zealous missionary. We all need the same amount of grace because the "currency" of our good works is debased and worthless before God."[1]

I struggle with chronic pain and nerve issues, none of which doctors have figured out. I've been through cancer three times (thankfully caught early).

It is only by God's grace that I have experienced complete peace through these things. I can't explain it apart from God. I think of the peace I experience now through physical trials, and marvel that this is a mere drop compared to the peace we will experience in heaven in our Father's presence and free from the effects of sin in this world.

As we begin this walk through Philippians, I pray that you will see God's grace and peace in new ways, be spurred to joy and thanksgiving and be inspired to extend God's gifts of grace and peace to others.

Day 1 ~ Philippians 1:1, 3-5, 7-8

Paul and Timothy, servants of Christ Jesus, to all the saints in Christ Jesus who are at Philippi, with the overseers and deacons:... I thank my God in all my remembrance of you, always in every prayer of mine for you all making my prayer with joy, because of your partnership in the gospel from the first day until now... It is right for me to feel this way about you all, because I hold you in my heart, for you are all partakers with me of grace, both in my imprisonment and in the defense and confirmation of the gospel.

I love my family and am close to them. I enjoy spending time with them. We support each other in the ups and downs. But even in the best of families, which not everyone has, there are fights and days we wish we weren't family. It is the same in God's family. We all have people at church that we love to be around and serve with, and those we wish would find a different church. Yes, I've thought that. Although we don't know all the interactions Paul had with the different people in the Philippian church, there were bound to have been some easy relationships and some difficult ones. Times of rejoicing and times of squashing rising frustration or flat out anger. Yet Paul's letter is not written to his star disciples in the church. His letter is not divided into sections for "Favorites" and "Tolerated." It is one letter to the whole church, and he calls them saints.

Paul began his letter with thanksgiving. I'm not talking about a quick "thnx" or "like". First, Paul's thanks to God for the Philippians was often. He says he thanks God in *all* his remembrances of and in *every* prayer for the Philippians. Paul was faithful not only in praying for the Philippians, but also in being thankful for them in specific ways. He was particularly thankful for their partnership with him in the gospel. The Greek word for partnership is *koinonia* – joint participation in a common interest or activity. In the Philippians' case, they were participating in the advancement of the gospel, and nothing was more important to Paul than knowing Christ and making Him known to others (Philippians 3:7-11). The Philippians supported Paul spiritually and financially as he worked to make the gospel known. They were with Paul from the "first" (not hanging on the sidelines waiting to see if he would be a success) and persevered with him until the end.

Koinonia is also a picture of intimate fellowship. The Philippians were not just co-workers that Paul tolerated because God said so. He loved his brothers and sisters in Christ (1:7), and it was *all* of them not just a few favorites. It is so easy for us to love only those who are easy to get along with.

Do you remember those times as a child when your mother told you to say "thank you" to someone? I do. Some of us may have stuck out our lip and turned away in refusal and some may have dutifully repeated, "thank you." I don't know how often I really meant it, but Paul did. He wasn't just being dutifully polite. In verse 4, Paul says his prayer is with JOY. This is joy as he sits in prison and possibly awaits execution. It is joy rooted in Christ and God's gift to Paul in the Philippians' partnership. Joy from their mutual receiving of God's grace. Joy from the Philippians' support in his suffering. It is joy that permeates his letter.

For Reflection: Start a list of people in your church to pray for (use your directory!). Don't just pick those that are easy to get along with or serve with but include those that irritate you or that you find uninteresting.

Beginning at the top of your list, thank God for at least one thing about each person. You might have to be more general with some you don't know as well. If you aren't sure, ask God to show you things to give thanks for and make a point of trying to talk to them this Sunday. Keep adding people and "thanks" to your list and go over your list weekly.

Day 2 ~ Philippians 1:6

And I am sure of this, that He who began a good work in you will bring it to completion at the day of Jesus Christ.

Have you ever been excited to start something new? Perhaps it is a home improvement project, cleaning out a closet or working on a craft. Maybe a new job or participating in a sport. It might even be a fantastic meal that you took extra portions of. You dig in with gusto, but then something derails you part way through. You lose your momentum. You lose your excitement. And whether it is immediate or more gradual, you quit. I am thankful that God does not lose heart when it comes to His work in me.

Paul writes that he is "sure of this." The Greek word for sure is *peithō*. It can also be translated as "persuaded or being confident." There is no doubt in Paul's mind that God will do what follows. His confidence is rooted in the character of God. God is completely capable (2 Timothy 1:12), He is with us (Psalm 23:4), and He is faithful (Psalm 33:4). We have that same assurance. The sin that each of us struggles with is not what defines us. The finished work of Christ does. Those sweet words "In Him" or "In Christ" that we find in Paul's letters are truths to grab onto.

The "good work" that was begun is salvation. This begins with God's work of justifying us through the atoning sacrifice and resurrection of His Son Jesus Christ. Ephesians 2:8-9 tells us that salvation is a gift of grace from God through faith. It is NOT a result of our works. That is cause for rejoicing. I don't know about you, but not a day goes by without some sinful thought, word or action in my life and usually more than one. Isaiah 64:6 declares that *all* my righteous deeds are like a polluted garment. So even on my best day, my works could not earn salvation. Thank you, Father, for saving me.

One commentator also ties the "good work" to *koinonia*, so the good work that God has begun is not just salvation but unity in the church as well. This idea connects it back to verse 5 when Paul highlights the Philippians' partnership with him. That partnership encompasses fellowship and intimacy.

But the good news does not stop there. Sometimes we can be stingy with what we give, but God never is. The second part of verse 6 adds that God will bring it to completion. The Greek for completion is *epiteleō* meaning "to bring to an end, to accomplish, to perfect" with a goal in mind. God always finishes what He starts in us at salvation, but what does that mean? The theological word is sanctification.

Sanctification is defined as "the continuing work of God in the life of the believer, making him or her actually holy."[2] Later on we will look more closely at this, but for now, out of our awe of God and thankfulness for what He has done, we walk in obedience by the enabling of the Holy Spirit. Our Heavenly Father is conforming us more and more to the image of Christ until we are complete on the day He returns for us. Even on our worst day, we can be assured that God is still working in us to conform us to the image of His Son. Rejoice!

For Reflection: First spend some time meditating on and being thankful for God's saving work in you. Think of what He saved you from and what He has saved you to.

Second, sometimes we can get discouraged feeling like we aren't becoming more like Christ and maybe are even going in the opposite direction. God often reminded Israel of what He had done for them, so that they would remember who God was (His character) and what He had done to encourage them to persevere in the present. Write down some of the changes God has done in you. Remember if you are saved, He has worked change! Then praise Him for His faithfulness and thank Him for the work He has done, is currently doing, and will ultimately complete.

"Our worst days are never so bad that you are beyond the reach of God's grace. And your best days are never so good that you are beyond the need of God's grace."[3]

Day 3 ~ Philippians 1:9-11

And it is my prayer that your love may abound more and more, with knowledge and all discernment, so that you may approve what is excellent, and so be pure and blameless for the day of Christ, filled with the fruit of righteousness that comes through Jesus Christ, to the glory and praise of God.

Today we get to peer into one of Paul's prayers. Why? Because Paul didn't just say he prayed for people, but he told them specifically how he prayed for them. One of the greatest blessings God gives me is knowing there are some who pray Scripture over me. To borrow words from the band Watermark, "'Cause you've been more than a friend to me/You fight off my enemies/You have spoken truth over my life."[4] I appreciate prayers for the temporal things in my life, but even more meaningful are the prayers for the eternal things.

Paul commences the prayer by asking God that the Philippians' love would "abound more and more." I enjoy studying theology and the Bible in general. To me, they often seem like the most important thing, but they are worthless without love (1 Corinthians 13:1-3). Jesus tells us in Mark 12:30-31 that the greatest commandment is to love God and the second is to love others. He doesn't say, "Get smart!" Love is first. Paul reminds us in Ephesians 4:15 that we are to "speak the truth in *love*."

Love combined with knowledge is able to see God with all of His attributes, and to see those around us as made in the image of God. Knowledge is the gospel, who we are in Christ, and what we do in response. Discernment is the effect of the knowledge or how to apply it. We are to discern between what is of the world (sin) and what is of God and choose those things that bring Him glory (v. 11).

Approve is an action verb. Paul didn't want the Philippians to be neutral in this world. They needed to stand for excellent things. In English we read excellent as an adjective, but in Greek, it is a verb meaning "to be better" or "to be of more value." Paul is praying for godly wisdom to know what things in life result in heavenly gain. Wisdom to live with a clear conscience before God. This is the process of sanctification, conforming us more and more to the image of Christ by making discerning choices regarding the things around us.

The result? Pure and blameless, filled with the fruit of righteousness. In Paul's day, vendors would try to sell cracked pots that had the cracks filled in with wax. Savvy shoppers would take the pots into the bright sunlight to check for wax-filled cracks. Pure describes a sun-tested pot without any cracks at all. Pure is also translated "sincere," referring to the idea of the winnowing process to remove chaff from wheat. This is a slow process not a quick fix. To be blameless is to be without offense towards God and man (Acts 23:1; 24:16; Ephesians 5:27). Fruit is evidence of sanctification (Romans 6:22), and it is the fruit of the Spirit (Galatians 5:22-23) that should show forth in every good work (Colossians 1:10). This fruit is only borne through Christ, and it is to God's glory not our own.

For Reflection: How do you pray for people? Do you pray for their sanctification? Are you specific? Are you speaking truth over their lives? Write out some of Paul's prayers and begin to pray them for others.

Day 4 ~ Philippians 1:12-14

I want you to know, brothers, that what has happened to me has really served to advance the gospel, so that it has become known throughout the whole imperial guard and to all the rest that my imprisonment is for Christ. And most of the brothers, having become confident in the Lord by my imprisonment, are much more bold to speak the word without fear.

Most of us have never been chained to another person. Most of us have probably never been in prison. However, most of us have felt as if we were trapped in a situation whether it be a frustrating job or co-worker, health issues, struggles in our marriage or with kids, or even conflict in ministry. I don't know how you respond, but some of my typical initial responses are whining and asking God to get me out! I want God to change my situation. Give me a new job. Heal me. Change my husband or kids. Quit ministering. Paul shows us a more excellent way.

We know from Acts 19:21 that Paul wanted to go to Rome (see Romans 1:13; 15:22-24). He planned it as part of his next journey, but God had a different plan. He did send Paul to Rome, but it was in chains. If anyone had reason to whine and ask for a way out, it was Paul (see 2 Corinthians 11:16-33 for a list of his sufferings). However, he doesn't dwell on his circumstances. He sums up all his sufferings simply as "what has happened to me." Four to seven years earlier, Paul had been in the Philippian jail, where he and Silas sang praises to God. That time God used an earthquake to open the cell doors. Now as in Philippi, Paul did not think of his own well-being but saw his chains as the open door to advance the gospel.

The Greek word for advance was a military term referring to army engineers who went before the troops, clearing the way to new territory. In these verses, we discover two ways this happened. First, Paul was chained to a guard twenty-four hours a day. The guards changed shifts approximately every six hours, which provided Paul a captive audience of four guards each day. They were present for everything he said, everything he dictated in his letters and every action he took. Not only did he have this captive audience, but they were the imperial guard – the emperor's own bodyguards not lowly grunt workers. Furthermore, Paul says "all the rest" which included every other remaining person in the imperial household and maybe even the entire city of Rome. Paul was blazing new gospel territory in the upper echelons of Roman society.

And it doesn't stop with Paul. Because of his bold witness, other believers in Rome became bold in speaking the gospel without fear. Paul paved the way for their witness. Remember, though, this all came about not because of a pleasant missionary trip to Rome but because of Paul's suffering and imprisonment. Paul chose praise and sharing the gospel over whining or trying to escape.

Furthermore, we know that Christ suffered physically, mentally and emotionally beyond what our human minds can really grasp for our salvation; that we could be in Him not left in our sin. I can't begin to imagine what Jesus felt when the Father forsook Him on the cross. Jesus who endured false accusations, mocking, beatings, the cruelest execution and more never once defended Himself, complained or used His power or authority to escape. How thankful I am that Christ's perfect record is now mine! It is reason to be bold in my faith.

For Reflection: Each of our trials is different, but we have all been through a trial or are currently in one. How did you or are you responding? Put off your whining and put on praise. God is sovereign over your circumstance. He is using it to conform you to Christ's image. You have Christ's perfect record. It is reason for praise. Write out specific ways you can use your circumstance to bear witness to the gospel and glorify God. You just might encourage others to do the same!

Day 5 ~ Philippians 1:15-18

Some indeed preach Christ from envy and rivalry, but others from good will. The latter do it out of love, knowing that I am put here for the defense of the gospel. The former proclaim Christ out of selfish ambition, not sincerely but thinking to afflict me in my imprisonment. What then? Only that in every way, whether in pretense or in truth, Christ is proclaimed, and in that I rejoice. Yes, and I will rejoice,

It seems like the church should be one big happy family. All unity. No fighting. But often it is where we see some of the worst division. We forget that the church is still entirely made up of sinners. We each still need God's grace every day, and we need to show that grace to those in the body. Paul again gives us that example.

Yesterday we saw him chained to a guard twenty-four hours a day, but still praising God and using the situation as an opportunity to advance the gospel. Today, we see Paul praising God despite people's efforts to afflict him by sharing the gospel from wrong motives. I tend to get defensive when people attack me. Paul was able to diminish self for God to be glorified. I recently finished studying Hebrews 11 and was struck by verses 36-38. These people are not even mentioned by name, like many others in the Hall of Faith. They aren't associated with miraculous events. These anonymous people are mentioned for their faith in extreme suffering. It convicted me of being a "glory-hoarder," the kind of people who were afflicting Paul.

Paul talks about one message, but two types of people sharing the message. Two different motives and attitudes. The latter group has the right motive of goodwill. They want to share their love for Christ. They also loved Paul. If he was willing to suffer in chains for the defense of the gospel, then they were willing to do their part to preach the gospel where they were.

The other group had sinful motives. They wanted to outdo Paul. They wanted him to suffer more, so they could be glorified. I'll be honest. I've had thoughts, words or actions that did the same towards a brother or sister in Christ. I dare say there is a "glory-hoarder" in each of us. I want recognition for my ministry efforts, and sometimes that may mean making someone else look bad for me to look better.

Paul could have responded defensively. He rightly could have confronted them about their sinful motives, but he was not focused on people. He was focused on the gospel. He was focused on God's glory above all else. He responded with grace and rejoicing because Christ was being proclaimed in both messages.

For Reflection: Spend some time praying and asking God to search your heart for your motives in the ministries you are involved in. Is your motive to bring glory to God or to self? Second, when people attack you, what is your response? Are you willing to put self aside for God to be glorified (assuming that their "message" is still advancing the gospel)? Are you willing to show others grace out of the grace God has given you?

Day 6 ~ Philippians 1:19-20

For I know that through your prayers and the help of the Spirit of Jesus Christ this will turn out for my deliverance, as it is my eager expectation and hope that I will not be at all ashamed, but that with full courage now as always Christ will be honored in my body, whether by life or by death.

This verse really follows the end of verse 18, "Yes, and I will rejoice, for I know that..." Paul rejoiced that the gospel was advanced, but we also see that his rejoicing is tied to the prayers of the Philippians on his behalf and to the help of the Spirit.

We know that Paul was a fervent prayer warrior especially for those in the churches he had planted. Here we see the flip side. We see Paul's gratitude for the Philippians' prayers for him. Paul recognized the value of their prayers and how God used them in his life. It gave him confidence.

Second Paul rejoiced because of the help of the Spirit. Note that he points to all three Persons of the Trinity throughout Philippians. The word for help in the Greek means "supply" or "a supplying." In ancient Greece, it was used to describe the funds given by an individual to hire singers for the city festival – a lavish donation. So when Paul says the "help of the Spirit," he is saying that he relies on the lavish resources of God given through the Spirit. He knows where his dependence lies.

The other word to explore here is deliverance. Some scholars say Paul expected to be released from prison, while others think he was referring to the mental or emotional deliverance of knowing that the gospel was being spread. I see in verse 20 that Paul talks about Christ being honored in his body, whether by life or death. Paul was content whatever God brought him – deliverance from prison or deliverance to the presence of God by death. Whatever the outcome, he saw it as a result of the Philippians' prayers and the help of the Spirit and counted it as deliverance.

I know I have many expectations and hopes. Most of them are very different from Paul's. His hope was to never be ashamed of the gospel or His Lord and Savior. His hope was that in life or death, he would honor Christ. Already in this first chapter of Philippians, we have perceived several times that Paul's focus was not on himself. It was always on the glory of God. He did not assume he would have full courage on his own. He knew that even the courage to stand firm came from God.

For Reflection: First, do you see the prayers of others for you as a gift? Do you share your burdens with others so they can pray for you as well as you praying fervently for them.

Second, do you daily see your need for the Spirit's help? Hourly? Minute by minute? We can do nothing good apart from God. Spend time in thanksgiving for the Spirit's indwelling and confess your need for His help.

Third, think about your hopes. Is honoring God etched on them?

Day 7 ~ Philippians 1:21-26

For to me to live is Christ, and to die is gain. If I am to live in the flesh, that means fruitful labor for me. Yet which I shall choose I cannot tell. I am hard pressed between the two. My desire is to depart and to be with Christ, for that is far better. But to remain in the flesh is more necessary on your account. Convinced of this, I know that I will remain and continue with you all, for your progress and joy in the faith, so that in me you may have ample cause to glory in Christ Jesus, because of my coming to you again.

How would you describe your life? Taxi Mom? Cooking, cleaning and laundry? A job outside the home? Your ministries? Paul asserted that for him "to live is Christ." Christ was his whole reason for being. As is the case for many, Paul did not have an identity in being a husband or father. He did work as a tent-maker as needed, and as a Pharisee, he was a very learned man. He had many social connections, yet he said, "to live is Christ." His identity and purpose were rooted in Christ.

Paul follows this with declaring "to die is gain." The Greek word for gain means "advantage." He knew it was better to depart and be in God's presence, to worship Him and to be fully united to Him, than it was to remain on earth. He was not afraid of death. He looked forward to it because he saw it as advantageous. In a game we may say one side has the advantage. That team is in a better position to win because of ability, coaching, equipment or fan support. To die in Christ means we have all the advantage. We have the ultimate win. Perfect fellowship with God. No more sin. No more suffering. No more tears. We have only the best forever. There is nothing more we can gain once we are in heaven.

So why was Paul torn? The phrase hard pressed means "to hold together with constraint or to compress." Paul loved the Philippians and his other spiritual children. He was thankful for their saving faith, but he also wanted to help them grow and mature. Paul said that remaining on earth meant fruitful labor. His fruitful labor was discipling them and continuing to glorify God while on earth.

In verse 24 Paul said it "is more necessary on your account" for him to remain. This was not a prideful stance on Paul's part. God could do the job without him. The Philippians would survive without him. It was really humbleness on Paul's part to put others' needs and what God had called him to before his own desire to be in glory. The word for necessary means "what one cannot do without, being indispensable, what is required by the circumstances."

Paul trusted God's sovereignty and wisdom for what was best for his life and the Philippians. He was willing to submit either way because ultimately, as we see in verse 26, Paul wanted the Philippians to glory in Christ. Whatever Paul did, he wanted it to result in God's glory. "'Glorifying' means feeling and thinking and acting in ways that reflect his greatness, that make much of God, that give evidence of the supreme greatness of all his attributes and the all-satisfying beauty of his manifold perfections."[5] For you and me glorifying God means showing others the grace He has abundantly shown us. It means loving others sacrificially the way Jesus loved us when He gave His own life for us, His enemies and sinners. It means growing in the fruit of the Spirit which reflect God's attributes. It means knowing that even when we miss the mark in glorifying Him, Christ always, perfectly glorified the Father, and He has given that record to you.

For reflection: Are there areas of your life you need to adjust so that they are about Christ not self? Take one at a time and write out specific ways you can make them about God's glory. For example: As a youth leader, my flesh wants the kids to like me. I want to be the awesome youth leader who is fun. The one they come to talk to. I am putting their approval of me above God's approval. God calls me to disciple them, to point them to Him. I can think of reasons to be thankful for other leaders that can also speak truth into their lives and love them instead of focusing on jealous thoughts.

Second, do you long for heaven? Do you see it as gain? Or are you caught up in this life. Paul said to be with Christ was far better. What do you need to loosen your hold on here to have this eternal perspective?

Day 8 ~ Philippians 1:27-28

Only let your manner of life be worthy of the gospel of Christ, so that whether I come and see you or am absent, I may hear of you that you are standing firm in one spirit, with one mind striving side by side for the faith of the gospel, and not frightened in anything by your opponents. This is a clear sign to them of their destruction, but of your salvation, and that from God.

Paul has shared his perspective on his circumstances; now he turns to the Philippians to encourage them in their circumstances. First, he encourages them to "let your manner of life be worthy of the gospel of Christ." The ESV translates the Greek *politeuomai* as "let your manner of life be." "Conduct your lives" would be a better translation. It meant to behave as a citizen, with a citizen's sense of dignity and responsibility. Paul is urging the Philippians to conduct their lives in a way that reflects the gospel. *Politeuomai* is where we get our words political and polite. The word manner is filled with meaning. The King James Version translates manner as "walk" or in an earlier translation "conversation." A *polis* was a small, close community of Greek citizens who were like-minded regarding rules and customs. This, along with patronage, was key to Greek society. Greeks took great pride in their duties and privileges as citizens. Paul uses this language to remind them of their heavenly citizenship. Their lives were to reflect that citizenship whether Paul was there to observe or not.

Next, he encourages them to stand firm. This word means "to persevere" or "to persist." The way they were to do that was through unity – one spirit, one mind. He further emphasizes this by the phrase "side by side." We get our word athlete from the Greek *sunathleō* which means "compete side by side." The prefix *sun* means "with" or "together." When used before *athleō*, *sun* strengthens the concept of unity. Paul was illustrating a team where everyone has their own role and gifts. All contribute to the team standing firm and advancing the gospel in the face of opponents. Ecclesiastes 4:9-12 details the benefits of unity especially in standing against an enemy.

Before we go on to the last part of verse 28, let's look at the word frightened. The Greek illustrates a striking picture of horses stampeding out of fear. Paul did not want the Philippians to react this way to opposition. In their unity in Christ, they could face the opposition with boldness.

Although there are many illustrations of unity in the New Testament, a well-known and effective one is the church as the body of Christ. If we were going into battle, we would want everything available to us in the physical body God gave us. We need our sight. We need our hearing. We need our arms and legs. We need our brain to think and lungs to breathe. Each component equips us better and gives us confidence that we have all our parts functioning for the battle. When we are unified with other believers, we have all the parts necessary for working together. We also have others standing beside us. Areas where I am weak, God has equipped my brother or sister in Christ. We have a common goal in the gospel. We are in Christ together. We need not fear.

Now what of this destruction? Christ already defeated Satan on the cross, but Satan likes to hinder us through fear tactics. The church's unity in the face of opposition points to Christ's coming judgment. It is a reminder that we are not the old man that shares their same doom. We are a new creation. We have been saved eternally. We are exhibiting proof of salvation.

For Reflection: In John 17:20-23 Jesus prays that believers would be unified just as He and the Father were one. That is serious unity! Paul says in these verses that unity is key to standing firm in the face of opposition. In Philippians 4, Paul addresses specific division in the Philippian church and pleads with the others in the church to help them be unified. Are you grasping the importance of unity in the body?

Think of your local church family. Are there those that you feel unified with? Why? Are there some you merely tolerate, perhaps ignore or are in outright contention with? Romans 12:18 tells us, "If possible, so far as it depends on you, live peaceably with all." John 13:35 states that others will know we belong to Christ by our love for each other. A divided church is not effective in the spread of the gospel or standing against evil. Where do you need to pursue unity with others? Is there a specific person? Situation? Do you need to ask forgiveness or overlook something in love? Take action!

Day 9 ~ Philippians 1:29-30

For it has been granted to you that for the sake of Christ you should not only believe in Him but also suffer for His sake, engaged in the same conflict that you saw I had and now hear that I still have.

There are two key things we need to keep in mind as we work through these two verses today. Let's start today with the word granted. The Greek *charizomai* translates "to grant as a favor" or "to give graciously." What follows is to be seen in light of this definition – it is a gracious favor to us. We also want to remember it is for the sake of Christ. It is for His glory.

What is this gracious favor that brings Christ glory? Paul says it is our faith by which we receive salvation. That is easy for us to see as good although day-to-day we may not always consciously think of it and be thankful. But wait! "but also suffer for His sake"? How is that a gracious favor to us and for His glory?

Acts 5:41 recounts to us the apostles response after being arrested, beaten and freed, "Then they left the presence of the council, rejoicing that they were counted worthy to suffer dishonor for the name." They rejoiced! Now their joy was not solely in the fact alone that they had suffered. It was in suffering for Christ's name. If Christ suffered for us, for our salvation, if He was beaten, despised, rejected and crucified, why would his followers not experience suffering for His name, for their firm stand for the gospel?

We know Paul suffered incredibly for the sake of the gospel. In Philippians 3:9-11 he says that all he suffered, all he lost was nothing compared to knowing Christ, to salvation, and to eternal life. Suffering for His name means that we are suffering for the right thing. Our suffering is bringing Him glory. If our purpose here on earth is to bring Him glory (1 Peter 4:11; 1 Corinthians 10:31), and our suffering can do that, we should rejoice in our suffering for His name.

Paul's exhortation came out of his own suffering that the Philippians had witnessed. They also witnessed Paul's steadfastness in the suffering. He spoke to them out of empathy not as an outsider. The word for *conflict* is where we get our word agony (Luke 22:44). It depicts a great struggle or battle. Paul did not minimize what the Philippians were going through. He recognized the agony of it.

Finally, we have the comfort of Christ Himself in our suffering. In Hebrews 4:15-16 we see Christ as our High Priest who can sympathize with our weaknesses. He was tempted in every way including suffering, but was without sin. Because of Christ, we can boldly come to the throne of grace, suffering and weak, and find mercy and grace for our time of need.

For Reflection: Are you suffering for Christ's sake? Do you view suffering as a gracious favor? An opportunity to glorify God and to be conformed to His image? Or do you complain? Take comfort that He has suffered for your sake, sympathizes with you and has made a way to come boldly to the throne of grace.

If you are not suffering for His sake, are there places you need to take a bolder stand for Christ?

Day 10 ~ Philippians 2:1-2

So if there is any encouragement in Christ, any comfort from love, any participation in the Spirit, any affection and sympathy, complete my joy by being of the same mind, having the same love, being in full accord and of one mind.

Throughout Philippians 1, we saw Paul point to Christ, His glory and the advancement of the gospel. In Chapter 2, Paul turns towards our next priority – others. This ordering echoes Mark 12:30-31, in which Jesus places first importance on loving God, and second on loving others. Paul is also building on the call to unity commanded in verse 1:27.

Don't let the "So if" fool you. Paul is being rhetorical regarding the four truths applying to believers. First, we do have encouragement in Christ. Luke 2:25 calls Christ the consolation. I cannot do justice to the full list of encouragements we have in Christ, but I will list a few. As believers, we are united to Christ (1 Corinthians 6:17). We are children of God and joint heirs with Christ (Galatians 4:6-7). We are justified (Romans 3:24; 5:1; Galatians 2:16-17). We are forgiven (Ephesians 4:32). We are complete in Christ (Colossians 2:10). We are new creations (2 Corinthians 5:17). We are not under condemnation anymore (Romans 8:1). Paul's letters are chock full of who we are *in Christ*. They overflow with this encouragement.

Second, we know that God so loved the world that He sent His only Son to die for our sins (John 3:16; Galatians 2:20). That is amazing love! Paul affirms in Romans 8:37-39 that there is NOTHING that can separate us from God's love. Matthew 27:51 gives us this glorious detail, "And behold, the curtain of the temple was torn in two, from top to bottom." For gentile Christians this may be hard to lay hold of. The curtain separated the Holy of Holies where God's presence dwelled. Only the High Priest could enter that Holy place and only once a year. That the curtain was torn completely in two, from top to bottom means that you and I can come boldly before the throne of grace into God's presence because of what Jesus the High Priest did once and for all on the cross (Hebrews 4:16). Did you hear that good news? Nothing can separate us from His love and from God Himself. That's comfort from love. We also know that God is the God of all comfort (2 Corinthians 1:3). Additionally, we have love from other believers (verse 2).

Third, "participation in the Spirit" can also be translated as "fellowship in the Spirit." The Greek word is *konoia* meaning "the sharing of things in common." Commentaries say that this can be our fellowship with the Spirit Himself as He indwells us, or our fellowship with other believers. Either way, we have support. We have fellowship. We are not alone.

Fourth, Paul talks about affection and sympathy or mercy. All Christians should know at least a bit of God's affection and mercy towards us from salvation as well as through our individual life experiences.

These four things give the foundation for the commands that follow particularly regarding unity with fellow believers and how we are to love them. The first command is to be "of the same mind." Paul is talking about unity not uniformity. We are to have the same attitudes, act in love towards each other and have the same purpose or one mind (glorify God and advance the gospel). Now, our unity is not uniformity. Uniformity means being all the same. God created each of us uniquely with different gifts and personalities. Differences make the parts of a body a whole, but it also opens the door for division. Paul's phrase of "full accord" comes from the Greek *syn* meaning "together with" and *psychos* meaning "soul." The idea is being united in spirit. Harmonious.

You may be thinking of so-and-so at your church. No harmony there! I have my so-and-so too. From our human perspective it seems impossible that we could ever have the same mind and be in full accord. I wish I could say I've nailed this, but I haven't. It is still a struggle, but I have also seen God work and bring unity in some of my impossible situations. First, I have to remember that God loved me while I was a sinner and His enemy (Romans 5:8, 10). He sought unity or reconciliation with me. I didn't make the first move. I couldn't make the first move. I couldn't even accomplish what that move required. Only God through Jesus on the cross could. Grace, that because it is shown to me, I can in Christ show to others. I remember my sin and my daily need for grace. I am no different than so-and-so.

Second, I begin to work at loving them unconditionally. Studying 1 Corinthians 13 has challenged me on my lack of love and God's perfect, unconditional love. As I started choosing to believe the best about so-and-so, bear with them, show kindness even if it isn't deserved (God's kindness to me isn't deserved!) and let go of having my own way, God changed my heart more and more. He has been equipping me to keep persevering even when so-and-so doesn't seem to respond. God reminds me that He works on different people in different ways at different times. I wasn't always where I am now, and I'm thankful He won't leave me here. I have to let go of my timetable for His work in their life. Not everyone will respond, but if we each have a unity in Christ mindset, unity will grow.

For Reflection: Paul starts verse 2 by saying, "complete my joy by" your unity. Have you ever thought of the impact you have on your church leaders when you are part of division in the body? Or have you thought of the joy that you can bring them by pursuing unity? What can you do this week to bring your church leaders joy through unity?

Day 11 ~ Philippians 2:3-4

Do nothing from selfish ambition or conceit, but in humility count others more significant than yourselves. Let each of you look not only to his own interests, but also to the interests of others.

Yesterday, we saw Paul's call to unity with our brothers and sisters in Christ. Today we will begin to explore the details of what he means. He starts by reminding us of verse 1:15 and those who preached from envy and rivalry. Although he was thankful that they were still getting the gospel out, here in chapter two he urges the Philippians to be different. He even expands this command to "do *nothing* out of rivalry or conceit." We need to put off these attitudes and motivations.

I love lists. I love that what I need to do is clear. I love being able to check off what I get done. The Biblical concept of putting off and putting on appeals to me. Put off this + Put on that = Godly result. However, it isn't usually that easy, and condensing this principle to an equation is a works or law mentality. I know that neither salvation or sanctification is by works, but often I, and maybe you too, default to a law mentality in our everyday life. I read my Bible today. Check. I prayed today. Check. I didn't get angry. Check. End of the day: God is pleased with me. This thinking reduces what Christ has done to nothing. If my completed checklist is what pleases God, then why did Jesus die for me? And what about all my righteousness being filthy rags?

I often start to twitch when things aren't going according to my list. And some of you might be twitching thinking I'm tossing out the need for obedience or the law. It's not the law that is the problem. It's not the principle of putting off and putting on that needs to change. It is my motivation. Your motivation. Have you ever thought about the standard format of Paul's letters? He typically spends the first half of his letter heaping on what God has done for us and who we are in Christ. The second half of the letter Paul then tells us how to respond in light of the first half. So, when we look at putting off sin and putting on godly responses, it is motivated by gratitude that Christ took the penalty for that sin we are putting off. It is motivated by thankfulness that the godly response we are putting on is how the Father already sees us in Christ. It is motivated by God's love for us and our love for Him not by a checkoff list.

The Greek for selfish ambition is the idea of campaigning for office. It is totally self-focused, self-promoting, self-loving, highlighting all your own good and ignoring your own sin. The Greek for conceit has the idea of empty pride. Pride that has no basis whatsoever.

Paul contrasts a heart of pride that promotes division with a humble heart that seeks unity. We know from Mark 12:31 that we already naturally love ourselves and look out for our own interests. Paul wants us to do even more for others than we do for ourselves. The word for significant means "to be above, superior in rank or more important." That is how we are to think of others.

So what does it mean to look out for their interests? Do we cater to their every whim? No, Paul is not talking about being a door mat. Humility was counter-cultural in Paul's day, and that is true today. As the great 19th-century preacher Charles Spurgeon wrote, "The apostle knew that, to create concord, you need first to beget lowliness of mind. Men do not quarrel when their ambitions have come to an end."

As we look to other's interests as more important, we have genuine concern for their needs. We want to bless them and be an encouragement. We are concerned about their well-being. We rejoice at good in their lives. This is active and takes effort to really consider the whole person and then act. In the next couple of days, we will see Christ's perfect example of humbling self to treat others as more significant.

For Reflection: Think of at least one person you can grow in unity with. On a sheet paper, make three columns. In one column write out what you think one or two of their needs, interests or perspectives is. In the next column, write out your interest in relation to that person and their need. In the third column, write out a choice you can make to put their interest ahead of your own. For example:

Other's Needs, Interests, Perspectives	**My Interests**	**My Choice**
	I have a daily list/schedule. I want to get through my list no matter what.	Set aside lesser priorities. Make special time for him.

Day 12 ~ Philippians 2:5-7

Have this mind among yourselves, which is yours in Christ Jesus, who, though He was in the form of God, did not count equality with God a thing to be grasped, but emptied Himself, by taking the form of a servant, being born in the likeness of men.

Today, we begin a passage that scholars consider a hymn, and which describes Jesus Christ as the perfect example of humility. This is one of my favorite passages in Scripture because it cuts me to the heart with how much He sacrificed to make me His own, and how unlike Him I am.

First, in verse 5, the word mind can also be translated as attitude depending on your version. The next phrase jumped out at me as I read it today, although I have read through Philippians numerous times – "which is yours in Christ Jesus." It can also be translated "which was also in Christ" and that is certainly a good translation. However, I do like the ESV. Not a day goes by in which I don't struggle with pride, but positionally because of Christ's atoning work, the perfect humility that Christ had (and has) is mine. I have His perfect humble record. Pause and sit there for a minute. Rejoice in that hope and good news. Yesterday I wrote out Day 11. That night at dinner with my niece, without even thinking, I chose my own interest over my niece's interest. I just had written about that, and I failed to live it. How thankful I am that when I come to God, He graciously forgives me and sees me with Christ's perfect record. I can go forward with hope that His humbleness is mine, and in Christ, I have the ability to walk in it.

Verse 6 is another mind-blowing truth. I don't think we can fully grasp all that Christ had in heaven, but picture all you know of heaven from Scripture. Angels twenty-four/seven worship God. No sin. No aches and pains. No crying. No angels betraying Him. It's perfect. Christ is God. He is equal with the Father. He deserves to be in Heaven and have all glory and honor. And yet, this verse says that He did not count that equality, that highest position of all authority and power, something to be grasped meaning He didn't cling to it as His right.

Our society today is full of this right and that right. People sue over their "rights," many of which shouldn't even be considered rights at all. How tightly we cling to what we think we deserve, and yet the One who really deserved all of Heaven, all glory and honor, willing emptied Himself – gave up what was rightfully His to take the form of a human servant.

Now that is another truth that should give us pause. Think of all that goes with our human bodies – hunger, tiredness, pain, clothes, need of shelter, daily relationships with sinners. Christ could have come as a full-grown man – a king with everything and everyone at His beck and call – but again, He chose humility. He came as a baby. A baby! Totally dependent on a mother to feed Him, change Him, take care of His every need. And not a child of privilege, but the child of an average couple in a stable. Christ did that for you. Hebrews 4:15 tells us that we have a High Priest who can sympathize with our weaknesses. That's because He came as that little baby in a stable to experience everything that we go through as humans. Wow!

For Reflection: When we are angry, hurt or jealous, it is usually because don't have something we think we deserve, or because we are getting something we think we don't deserve. We are clinging to what we consider our rights. What are you clinging to in pride that you need to let go of in humility to foster unity with others?

As an extra reflection, go back through verses 1-5 and make a table of "If (Any)" on one side and "Then (Complete my joy by)" on the other side and fill it in. The "Ifs" help us put into perspective the "Thens" that Paul calls us to walk in.

Day 13 ~ Philippians 2:8

And being found in human form, he humbled Himself by becoming obedient to the point of death, even death on a cross.

Did you dwell on Christ's humility and all He did for you yesterday? I hope so. It's something we should dwell on often and be thankful. Today we will see that Christ humbly did even more for us.

Verse 8 reminds us again that Christ was "found" in human form. Although still fully God, He was also fully human. The death He died and all that preceded it was not somehow lessened for Him as the Son of God. Physically, He experienced everything just the way you or I would.

Paul follows by saying that Christ humbled Himself by becoming obedient. *Humbled* means "to make low." Christ willingly chose this obedience. How often are we humbled by others, by God or by our own poor choices? Not the way to be humbled. It is better when the humbling comes by our own willingness because we are obeying God.

Christ's obedience to His Father extended to the very act of surrendering His own life, and it wasn't just any death. Paul elaborates that it was death on a cross, the most humble way to die at that time. It was referred to as a cursed, painful and shameful way to die (Deuteronomy 21:23). I won't go into all the details, but if you want an accurate picture of all Christ suffered for you in His death, watch the *Passion of the Christ*. Christ chose the pain, the humiliation, the mockery and being a public spectacle for you and for me.

Paul gives us the perfect model of being humble and putting others' interests above our own. I cannot think of any time in my life that I have shown that degree of humbleness or have been faced with that severe a circumstance to choose as Christ did. I know there are many who do face incredible persecution for their faith today, but for most of us, our situations will never compare. Yet, we still often choose our own interests above humility. We know what Christ has done for us, and we still struggle with lesser sacrifice in our own lives.

Praise God for His grace! Even in our weak moments, He perfectly obeyed in our place, and lavishes His love and forgiveness on us. He gave us His Spirit to indwell us, strengthen us, and equip us to walk in grateful obedience.

For Reflection: The Father called Jesus to be our atoning sacrifice. In His word, we see many things that He calls us to in obedience. Is there a situation or a specific command that you have been unwilling to fully, humbly obey? What can you do to follow Christ's example?

Day 14 ~ Philippians 2:9-11

Therefore God has highly exalted Him and bestowed on Him the name that is above every name, so that at the name of Jesus every knee should bow, in heaven and on earth and under the earth, and every tongue confess that Jesus Christ is Lord, to the glory of God the Father.

We have a therefore to begin these verses. Yesterday we saw Christ's humble obedience culminating in His willing, sacrificial death. "Therefore, God has highly exalted Him." Highly exalted is the Greek word *hyperypsoō* meaning "exalted beyond measure." This is fitting of God who is transcendent of all measurements. Christ returns to His glorious status that was His before He humbled Himself to come to earth in human form.

The Father also bestows on Christ the name that is above every name. YWHW was the name above all names for God for the Jews. It was so holy that they would not even utter it, but substituted Lord for it. With Jesus' name, it is not so much the sound of the name as the authority behind the name.

There is a scene in *The Lion King* where the hyena "bad guys" talk about how they hate lions, and especially the king of lions, Mufasa. Just saying Mufasa's name leaves them both shaking. This is a dim example. The hyenas are afraid of Mufasa and his power not in awe of Him, but I imagine on that day when every knee bows and every tongue confesses that Jesus is Lord, that it will give us chills. The Name alone will put us in awe of Christ like never before.

One of the incredible things about this day is that it says *every*. This echoes the same phrase used in Isaiah's prophecy of the worship offered to the Lord Himself in Isaiah 45:23. "In heaven" means all those in heaven will bow and confess. "On earth" means that all the living will bow and confess." "Under the earth" means that all the dead and lost will confess. "Every tongue" means that every nation and language will confess. All will publicly confess Christ as the exalted, omnipotent Redeemer who is Master over everything.

And not only is the Son exalted, but honor of Him will ultimately bring glory to the Father. This is just the beginning of an eternity of glorifying God and praising His Name, the beginning of amazing, unending worship. What a day to look forward to!

Every time I read these verses, I long for this day when every knee will bow and every tongue confess that Jesus is Lord. Finally, all that is due in worship to Christ will be His including my own now perfect honoring of Him. I won't be distracted. There won't be sin to break my fellowship with God. Just perfect worship of our Amazing Lord and Savior, God and Father.

For Reflection: The good news is we don't have to wait for that day to worship God. We can do it every day in songs of praise, in words of gratitude, in obedient lives, in prayer and in reading His Word. What can you do in your daily routine to glorify God more?

Day 15 ~ Philippians 2:12-13

Therefore, my beloved, as you have always obeyed, so now, not only as in my presence but much more in my absence, work out your own salvation with fear and trembling, for it is God who works in you, both to will and to work for His good pleasure.

"Therefore," in light of Christ's humble example and atoning death, Paul calls us to obedience. Interesting that their obedience is to be in his presence or his absence. Have you ever asked a child to do something, left the room only to come back and find they did nothing while you were gone? Or maybe you are in the room. They keep peeking to see if you are watching before they obey. Adults aren't always that different from children in behavior. Paul did not want their obedience to be motivated by fear of a watchful dad. He wanted their motivation to be a heart of thankfulness and love for their Lord and Savior.

Now we get to the tricky part of these verses. Some would say that the phrase "work out your own salvation" supports a works salvation – that we earn our own salvation by our good works. This is true of all other world religions. Before we jump on that bandwagon, let's look at the whole of Scripture. We don't want to isolate a verse from what the rest of Scripture says.

In Isaiah 64:6 we see that even our best good deeds are as filthy rags before a holy God. We know from Romans 3:23 that we have all sinned and fallen short of God's glory. Galatians 3:10 says that if we are to rely on our works for salvation, we would have to keep the *whole* law. There is only One person I know who has done that. Ephesians 2:8-9 tells us that it is by grace we are saved *not* by our own works so that no one can boast. There are many more verses I could list, but I hope you are seeing that when we look at topic within all of Scripture, it is pretty clear that we could never be good enough or do enough to earn our own salvation. And if we could, why would Jesus have willingly humbled Himself to come to earth in the form of a human baby, suffer and die on a cross? His amazing act of love would be a waste.

So how do we interpret this verse? Salvation is fully redemptive. It is a completed act. Remember, Paul was writing to the Philippian church as partners in the gospel (1:5). He believed they were already saved. I'm going to jump to verse 13 for a moment. It says that it is God who works in us. If it were not for God working in us first, we would never be able to work out what He has done in us. Our works are evidence of our salvation. We daily show by our obedience that we belong to God. Jesus said that a good tree will bear good fruit (Matthew 7:17-18). James reiterates this idea that our works are evidence of our faith (James 2:14ff). So in these verses, Paul is again talking about our sanctification. We walk in obedience, we bear good fruit, and we become conformed more and more to the image of Christ.

How are we to do this? With fear and trembling. Your first thought may be of a spider or a snake or maybe bungee jumping. Snakes are my fear. We might run away screaming or trying nonchalantly to kill the spider while your heart is racing. But the fear Paul commands us to have is an awe and reverence for God. It is a trembling that joyfully looks to encountering the glory of God. That definition affects the context of working out our salvation. If we are trying to earn our own salvation, we would agonize whether we had satisfied the almighty ruler of everything. But if our motivation is an awe of God for what He has done and who He is, then we joyfully want to do what pleases Him.

For Reflection: Verse 12 says your *own* salvation. We often get focused on what we think others should be doing. What area of obedience do you need to work on in your own life?

Day 16 ~ Philippians 2:14-16

Do all things without grumbling or disputing, that you may be blameless and innocent, children of God without blemish in the midst of a crooked and twisted generation, among whom you shine as lights in the world, holding fast to the word of life, so that in the day of Christ I may be proud that I did not run in vain or labor in vain.

Stick with me. This may be a challenging day. Right away, as far as our daily verses go, Paul tells us to do *all* things without grumbling or disputing. Right there I know I want to interject, "Paul, you don't know this person I serve with" or "You haven't worked at my job." Or, or, or…our list could go on. But pause for a minute to think on and about Paul's life – all his travels, shipwrecks, beatings, imprisonments, oppositions, stonings, betrayals. In chapter 4 we will read about Paul's contentment in *all* circumstances (and he lists several not so good ones). He personally knows how hard it is to "do all things without grumbling or disputing."

The language Paul uses in the Greek takes us back to the Israelites wandering in the desert (Exodus 15:24; 16:7-9). We need to remember that any grumbling and disputing is always against God. We are questioning His goodness, His love, His wisdom, His sovereignty. We are telling Him that He screwed up. He made a mistake placing us alongside so and so. That our boss is outside God's control. That we really know better than He does how to handle our situation. We may never say those things to God, but that is what our grumbling and disputing is really saying.

The Greek word for grumble, *goggysmos*, means to murmur or mutter, but it also can mean a secret debate or a secret displeasure. However, it is never secret from God. The Greek for dispute is *dialogismos*, which we get our word dialogue from. It is questioning what is true. There are times we go to God with questions, but it is with a heart that is submissive to Him and trusting of Him. A grumbling and disputing heart is against God.

God in His grace explains through Paul why we should do all things without grumbling or disputing. He wants to work in us, sanctify us, make us blameless, innocent and without blemish, so that we stand out in the world as different. Others will see our good deeds and glorify God (Matthew 5:16). The word blameless carries the idea of undeserving of any censure. We are not perfect, but we try not to give anyone reason to rebuke us. If we do sin, we ask forgiveness. The word for blemish is interesting. The Greek is *amōmos*. Momus, a Greek god, would find fault with everyone and with everything. This phrase could be interpreted, "Walk so circumspectly that Momus himself may have no occasion to fault you."

We have the what to do and the why to do it. Now the how: we hold fast to the word of life. The Word is our anchor. It is the same Greek word in John 1:1 used to describe Jesus being the Word. I need Jesus. We need Jesus. We hold fast to the Word, but we can also hold it out for the world to see like a light. We want to direct others to Jesus.

For Reflection: What do you tend to grumble and dispute about? Is your grumbling habitual? Confess your complaining to God. Then write down things to be thankful for in each of the things you tend to grumble about. The next time you feel like grumbling, get your thankful list out and choose that instead.

Day 17 ~ Philippians 2:17-18

Even if I am to be poured out as a drink offering upon the sacrificial offering of your faith, I am glad and rejoice with you all. Likewise you also should be glad and rejoice with me.

In verses 2:5-11, Paul showed us how Christ poured Himself out as an offering for us. In the Old Testament the offerings made by the Israelite priests were a God-given precursor of the sacrificial life and death of Christ. Every morning and evening the priests were to offer sacrifices of a lamb, grain and wine as a symbol of joy (Exodus 29:38-42; Numbers 28:1-8). God allowed the priests to take a portion of the food offerings, but the drink offering was completely poured out on the altar. In Hebrews 12:2, we see the tie to the symbol of joy in the Old Testament offerings. "…who for the *joy* that was set before Him endured the cross, despising the shame, and is seated at the right hand of the throne of God." What a beautiful picture of Jesus' perfect, complete, joyful offering on our behalf.

In verse 17, Paul connects the example of Old Testament sacrifices and Jesus' own sacrifice to his own life and that of the Philippians. Paul uses the present tense in the Greek of being poured out. He may be thinking of his current suffering or the possibility of martyrdom for his faith. Either way, he rejoices that God would use him as an offering (again that tie to the symbol of joy in the drink offering).

Paul further connects the image of a drink offering to the sacrificial offering of the Philippians' faith. He is referring to the gifts that they sent him (4:10, 15-18). The Philippians had supported Paul when no other church did. As soon as they were able, they sent him gifts through Epaphroditus, and they had partnered with him in the gospel (1:5). Paul saw this all as an offering reflective of their faith. In 4:18, he calls their gifts "a fragrant offering, a sacrifice acceptable and pleasing to God." Another reason he could rejoice is he knew this was evidence of fruit increasing in their life (4:17). Paul had joy in the spiritual growth of the Philippians.

We often try to avoid sacrifice and suffering. Paul calls us to see the joy in submission in suffering and to encourage the Philippians (and us) that they could experience the same joy Jesus and he had no matter what the circumstances because it brings glory to God.

For Reflection: Are you willing to be poured out as a drink offering for the glory of God, or do you pour out only what is comfortable? Do you choose joy in your suffering because it is an opportunity to glorify God and communicate His goodness, faithfulness, love and sovereignty, or do you complain and ask God to remove your circumstance?

Day 18 ~ Philippians 2:19-24

I hope in the Lord Jesus to send Timothy to you soon, so that I too may be cheered by news of you. For I have no one like him, who will be genuinely concerned for your welfare. For they all seek their own interests, not those of Jesus Christ. But you know Timothy's proven worth, how as a son with a father he has served with me in the gospel. I hope therefore to send him just as soon as I see how it will go with me, and I trust in the Lord that shortly I myself will come also.

I have been in Youth Ministry for almost thirty years. Many of the teens in the youth groups over the years have become like my own kids. My husband and I invest in them. I'm thankful that so many of them have become good friends as they've grown older. If you've been involved in discipleship at all, you can probably understand that one of the greatest joys in my life is seeing one of our kids make their faith their own. They graduate, leave home and choose to follow God. It delights my heart to see them involved in ministry, serving, growing and raising their own children to love God. I'm guessing this is some of what Paul felt about Timothy.

So far we have seen examples of Christ's and Paul's humble attitude in putting other's interests above their own. Today we get a glimpse into Timothy's humble service. Timothy was born to a Jewish Christian mother and a Greek father. Paul probably met him on his first missionary journey, and Timothy became like a son to him. Paul mentions Timothy twenty-four times throughout his letters. At the writing of Philippians, Timothy had ministered with Paul about ten years.

Paul tells the Philippians that he has no one like Timothy – someone who is equal in soul or likeminded. Why? What made Timothy special? We glean a couple reasons here. The first is that Timothy will be genuinely concerned about the Philippians' welfare. The word genuinely carries the idea of it being natural to Timothy. Caring for others was not an effort for him. He was willing and sincere in promoting other's interests.

In conjunction with this, Paul contrasts Timothy with the others who are all seeking their own interests. Timothy seeks the interests of Jesus. We don't know exactly who "they all" were. It would not have meant every other minister of the gospel since in verses 25-30 Paul commends layman Epaphroditus, and Paul would not have characterized Peter and the apostles as seeking their own interests. However, it is a sad commentary that seeking their own interests described most of the other ministers in comparison to Timothy. Timothy stood out as following Christ's example described in verses 6-8. Timothy was concerned about the things that concerned Jesus.

Next, Paul states that Timothy has proven his worth, and the Philippians were witnesses to this. Timothy had proven himself by his faithful service side-by-side with Paul. He traveled with Paul. Served with Paul in the gospel. Suffered with Paul. Even stayed near him when Paul was in prison. This was over the course of ten years. Timothy was faithful. We can see why Paul called Timothy his "true child in the faith" (1 Timothy 1:2) and "my beloved child" (2 Timothy 1:2).

The other element to note in these verses is the reason Paul was sending Timothy to the Philippians. Paul loved the Philippians (1:7-8). It had been awhile since Epaphroditus had come to him from Philippi, and Paul longed to know how the Philippian church was doing. Their well-being brought him joy (2:19). Paul could not go himself as he was imprisoned although we see at the end of verse 24 that Paul hoped to see them again. In the meantime, Paul wanted a personal report from Timothy, the one he trusted most to represent him in his absence.

For Reflection: As you search your own heart, does concern for others come naturally to you? Are you willing to serve those God places in your life? Are your interests those of Christ's? If not what steps do you need to take to cultivate that kind of heart? In doing so, you will love others, glorify God and bless your spiritual leaders.

Day 19 ~ Philippians 2:25-30

I have thought it necessary to send to you Epaphroditus my brother and fellow worker and fellow soldier, and your messenger and minister to my need, for he has been longing for you all and has been distressed because you heard that he was ill. Indeed he was ill, near to death. But God had mercy on him, and not only on him but on me also, lest I should have sorrow upon sorrow. I am the more eager to send him, therefore, that you may rejoice at seeing him again, and that I may be less anxious. So receive him in the Lord with all joy, and honor such men, for he nearly died for the work of Christ, risking his life to complete what was lacking in your service to me.

We have already looked at humble examples in Jesus, Paul and Timothy. Today we study our fourth example of someone who humbly puts others' needs above his own. This passage is the only place we read of Epaphroditus. We know he was a Gentile from the church in Philippi sent to Paul possibly to take him a gift (verse 30), and possibly consult with him on church issues and/or to minister to him in prison (verse 25b).

Paul calls Epaphroditus his brother (verse 25) revealing the fellowship they had in the gospel. He also calls him a fellow worker denoting Epaphroditus' work in furthering the gospel. Third, Paul calls him a fellow soldier showing his perseverance through suffering, in this case his illness almost to death, all for the sake of the gospel.

Fourth, Paul says that Epaphroditus was the Philippian church's messenger and minister to Paul's need. Epaphroditus brought news of the Philippians to Paul. We know from chapter 1 and 4:1 how much Paul loved the Philippian church, so this was a blessing to him to have word of those he loved. As a minister, Epaphroditus likely brought a gift from the Philippian church ("minister to my need."), as Paul mentions specifically in 4:18. In verse 30 Paul said that Epaphroditus completed what was lacking in the Philippians' service to him. This does not mean that the Philippians were inadequate, but that Epaphroditus was their only way to get help or a gift to Paul.

Fifth, we know that Epaphroditus was sick and almost died (verse 27). Although we don't know what illness he had, we know it was due to his work for Christ and in coming to see Paul, a possible 750-1200 mile trek (depending on route) without the aid of airplanes or cars. We know that God had mercy on Epaphroditus and healed him (verse 27), and that it was also a mercy to Paul to spare Epaphroditus as he was such a valuable partner in the Gospel. The Philippians had somehow heard of his illness and near death causing them worry for him, and thus caused Epaphroditus distress. The word for distress means a "great anguish". It is the strongest of three words used in the New Testament for distress or depression. Epaphroditus was more concerned about the Philippians than he was his own health.

For these reasons Paul thought it necessary to send Epaphroditus back to the Philippian church. The word for necessary means "indispensable" or "what one cannot do without." Paul felt strongly about sending Epaphroditus home. It would be cause for the Philippians to rejoice (verse 28) and to relieve both Epaphroditus and Paul of their sorrow of knowing the Philippians were worried about Epaphroditus (verse 28b).

For Reflection: In verse 29, Paul tells the Philippian church to receive Epaphroditus with joy and to honor him. Do you think of your church leaders with joy? What can you do to show them honor and your gratefulness for their work in serving Christ in the body?

Day 20 ~ Philippians 3:1-3

Finally, my brothers, rejoice in the Lord. To write the same things to you is no trouble to me and safe for you. Look out for the dogs, look out for the evildoers, look out for those who mutilate the flesh. For we are the circumcision, who worship by the Spirit of God and glory in Christ Jesus and put no confidence in the flesh —

"Finally" –The Greek word means "for the rest of things that remain." Paul is introducing a new section. He is going to deal with the Judaizers, who falsely taught that Gentile Christians needed to submit to Jewish rules and regulations in order to be saved. He commences his refute with "rejoice in the Lord." Paul will repeat this in 4:4 as well. When I think of someone giving me a pile of rules to conform to versus the freedom I have in Christ, I rejoice at freedom. This intro may be Paul's way of reminding the Philippians of who they are in Christ, and it is not about obeying man-made laws. As we focus with gratitude on what Christ has done for us, and who we are in Him, we are less likely to be drawn away by teaching that is contrary to the Gospel.

Paul follows the command to rejoice by warning the Philippians he is going to repeat things he had told them in person when he was in Philippi. Paul says it is for their safety to have it repeated. I don't know about you, but I too easily forget things whether the items on my grocery list or gospel truths. I need to be reminded. Hence, I write out my grocery list. I write down spiritual truths and stick them up in places I see every day. We need to flood our minds with truth continually.

Over the next several days we will look at the details of what Paul considered of vital importance to repeat, but for today we note his warning. He uses strong words to urge the Philippians. He wants them to be discerning of the dogs. Dogs were considered unclean (see Revelation 22:15). The Gentiles used the term in a derogatory way, as did the Jews (Mark 7:27-28). It was also a metaphor for one who had an impure mind. Paul adds to his description with "evildoers," someone of a destructive nature. Judaizers thought they were doing good, but they really did evil in adding works to salvation. Paul's final description is "those who mutilate the flesh." Circumcision, one of the Judaizers rules, was of no value in itself. It was simply mutilation. Paul has more harsh words in Galatians 5:12 where he says that he wishes that circumcisers, those leading others astray by requiring works, would emasculate themselves. Paul viewed the Judaizers as a serious defilement of the Gospel.

In comparison, he reminds the Philippians of who they are. They, and we, have the true circumcision of the heart. We are characterized by worshipping by the Spirit of God. The Old Testament required outward signs of worship with regulations on meat, drinks, cleansing, etc. We have the Spirit indwelling us. Our worship comes from inside, from a heart changed by God. We glory or boast in Christ, and His atoning sacrifice that saves us. We do not have confidence in our flesh or in our works to save us or earn us ongoing favor with God.

For Reflection: What gospel truths do you need reminding of? Write out those verses and post them around your home or work area. Read them every day. Rejoice in what God has done for you!

Day 21 ~ Philippians 3:4-6

Though I myself have reason for confidence in the flesh also. If anyone else thinks he has reason for confidence in the flesh, I have more: circumcised on the eighth day, of the people of Israel, of the tribe of Benjamin, a Hebrew of Hebrews; as to the law, a Pharisee; as to zeal, a persecutor of the church; as to righteousness under the law, blameless.

Yesterday we established that we who truly belong to Christ do not trust in our own works for salvation. We glory in Christ and His atoning work. Today we will review Paul's impressive pedigree as a Jew. He had more reasons than most people to have confidence in his own works or human standing, if that is what God valued. However, we'll see what God, and Paul, actually value tomorrow.

Paul's first pedigree point is being circumcised on the eighth day. Circumcision was the primary regulation that Judaizers pushed on Gentile Christians. Paul emphasizes that he was circumcised according to the exact method in Genesis 17:12. Paul then moves on to his lineage. By saying that he is of the people of Israel, he is stating that he is a pure Hebrew, born through the line of Abraham, Isaac and Jacob. He further underlines this by declaring he is a Hebrew of Hebrews. This means that his lineage is totally pure. There is no Gentile blood mixed in.

He refines this even more by noting which of the twelve tribes of Jacob he is from, the tribe of Benjamin. Joseph and Benjamin were Jacob's two favored sons because they were the sons born of Rachel, the wife he loved most. Israel's first king came from the tribe of Benjamin, and the tribe of Benjamin was faithful to King David when Absalom tried to take the kingdom from David.

Next Paul switches to a spiritual pedigree by describing himself as a Pharisee. Pharisees occupied the pinnacle position in Judaism. There was no one higher in the spiritual chain. Paul studied under one of the leading Pharisees of the time, Gamaliel (Acts 22:3), he was the son of a Pharisee (Acts 23:6), and he was from the strictest sect of Pharisees (Acts 26:5). Paul was such a zealous Pharisee that he persecuted the Christian church. Jews were opposed to the Christian church as they did not believe that Jesus was the Messiah. Although his beliefs were false, he was all for pursuing what he believed was truth. He was anything but nominal. Paul's final appeal to his pedigree is his obedience to Jewish law. He claims he was blameless. No one would have been able to find fault with him in relation to Jewish law.

Wow! That is quite a pedigree. I know my pedigree doesn't even come close, but we will see tomorrow that Paul dismisses it all. When God got a hold of his heart on the road to Damascus, He radically changed Paul's priorities.

For Reflection: We may know in our head that we can't earn salvation or God's favor with our works, but we often behave as if we can. What things in your pedigree do you tend to look to for your standing with God or others?

Day 22 ~ Philippians 3:7-8

But whatever gain I had, I counted as loss for the sake of Christ. Indeed, I count everything as loss because of the surpassing worth of knowing Christ Jesus my Lord. For His sake I have suffered the loss of all things and count them as rubbish, in order that I may gain Christ...

I have been doing accounting for many years. When I look at a balance sheet, I want the assets (positives) to outweigh the liabilities (negatives). We call this being in the black. We have a positive balance. Paul uses accounting language in these verses. His impressive pedigree (that we looked at yesterday) puts him exceedingly in the black from a human perspective. His plusses far exceed any negatives. This is where we want to be, right?

But then we come to verse 7. Paul declares that whatever gain he had, he now counts as loss. He took all those plusses and put them on the liability side. He is now in the red as an accountant would say. Why? Why would he do this? Paul's answer is "for the sake of Christ." What was of value to Paul was what brought glory to Christ. Paul considered what he gained of far more value than what he lost. The word for knowing indicates a personal, intimate knowledge that comes through experience. It's this relationship with Christ that was of exceptionally more value to Paul.

Paul elaborates that he not only counts his pedigree as loss, but he counts everything as loss compared to "the surpassing worth of knowing Christ."

For Paul, there is nothing this world has that compares to intimate relationship with Christ. He also knows that his human-perfect pedigree will never be enough. Paul lost many things for the sake of Christ – his family, his earthly inheritance, his standing in the community, his friends, stability, safety, comforts, steady income, liberty and ultimately his life – but none of this mattered to knowing Christ.

We also have Jesus' example that we saw in 2:6-11. Jesus had equality with the Father and the Spirit, but He didn't hold onto that. He was willing to suffer that loss and the loss of all He had in heaven to come to earth as a baby, live as a human with all that entailed, suffer and die for us.

The word "count" is present tense. Daily Paul is considering those human plusses as loss. It is not a one-time act. Daily we need to remember that the temporal things of this world are not what is of true value.

Paul continues by saying that for Christ he suffered the loss of all things. It is by Christ's loss alone that Paul was able to lose everything and yet rest in knowing it was gain. Paul's suffering was not because he lost things of earthly value. His suffering was from persecution in choosing Christ. From a human perspective, Paul gave up all this great stuff and he gained suffering, but again he says he counts them as rubbish – garbage or dung. Paul's perspective is amazing. Counter-cultural. Now this doesn't mean we aren't thankful for the good gifts God gives us, but we don't hold tightly to them, and we live knowing that what we have in Christ far surpasses those good, earthly gifts. Tomorrow we will see more of what Paul, and we, have gained in Christ.

For Reflection: Do you view your relationship with Christ as gain? Do all other things in your life pale in comparison? It is easy to get focused on temporal things especially when they are good. What temporal things do you need to loosen your grip on, so you can grow in intimacy with Christ?

Day 23 ~ Philippians 3:9-11

And be found in Him, not having a righteousness of my own that comes from the law, but that which comes through faith in Christ, the righteousness from God that depends on faith — that I may know Him and the power of His resurrection, and may share His sufferings, becoming like Him in His death, that by any means possible I may attain the resurrection of the dead.

In these verses, Paul paints an amazing picture. He begins by continuing his thought of gaining Christ, and that he, Paul, would be found in Him. "In Him" – two little words that hold a wealth of meaning. In his letters, Paul uses the phrase "in Christ" or "in the Lord" over 160 times. We cannot look at all these instances today, but *Found In Him* by Elyse Fitzpatrick draws out the fullness of what it means to be in Him.[6] Paul used language here that echoes Numbers 35:25 describing the cities of refuge. If someone had committed what we would call manslaughter, an unplanned, unintentional killing, they could flee to a city of refuge and be safe from any punishment as long as they stayed within the city's boundaries. When we are found in Christ, we are safe and protected. Christ took the penalty for us. We are free in Him.

Not only did Christ take our penalty on Himself at the cross, His righteousness was imputed or credited to those who are found in Him (2 Corinthians 5:21; 1 Corinthians 1:30). More accounting language. In Christ you have been given His perfect, spotless, sinless record. No wonder Paul counted all the other things in his life as loss! What he gained was something he could never have attained on his own. And all that God asks from us for this great gain is faith in Christ's atoning work (Ephesians 2:8-9). This leaves me in awe, gratitude and full of love for my Savior.

But wait! There's more in Christ. Paul says, "that I may know Him," and he lists two of the ways we can know Christ more fully. The word for know, in addition to the idea of understanding something, is used for relations between a husband and wife. Paul is referring to an intimate, personal knowledge of Christ. Not general facts. First, he says that we can know the power of His resurrection. If we are in Him, we have the same Spirit who raised Christ from the dead indwelling us. The power of His resurrection means that we have life. We are free from sin. We are justified. Christ's resurrection brought power over sin and death.

Second, we can share in His sufferings and become like Him in His death. Paul is talking about daily dying to our sin. Christ defeated our sin once for all on the cross and took the penalty for us, but until we are glorified in heaven, we still will daily battle with sin. We must put it to death and put on the things of God (Ephesians 4:22-24; Colossians 3:5-15). This daily dying to sin can mean suffering. It is not always easy to put off our sin. This lifestyle may also mean persecution. Being like Christ in His death also means that we will one day be resurrected and glorified. Paul eagerly looked forward to and longed for heaven. Any suffering here he viewed as a light and momentary affliction (2 Corinthians 4:17-18).

For Reflection: We often think of Christ's taking our sin and paying the penalty for it, but I think we forget that in Him, we were also given His righteousness. When you sin, are you weighed down by guilt? Is it hard to believe that God has forgiven you? Yes, we need to recognize that sin against a holy God is serious, but we can also rest in God's gracious gift to us of Christ's righteousness. God does not look on you and see your sin. He sees His Son's perfect record. That is cause for rejoicing and thankfulness.

Day 24 ~ Philippians 3:12-14

Not that I have already obtained this or am already perfect, but I press on to make it my own, because Christ Jesus has made me His own. Brothers, I do not consider that I have made it my own. But one thing I do: forgetting what lies behind and straining forward to what lies ahead, I press on toward the goal for the prize of the upward call of God in Christ Jesus.

Here, Paul switches from accounting to athletic language. In verses 8-11, Paul informed us of what was most important to him. He continues that thought process in comparing the pursuit of knowing Christ to competing in a race. In Philippi, Macedonia, the Philippians would have been familiar with the Greek (Panhellenic) Games in which you were required to be a citizen to compete. You did not compete to earn your citizenship. This is important background along with what we already studied in verses 1-11. Paul does not switch to a works salvation in these verses. We already have our citizenship in heaven because of faith in Christ (verse 9), so we press on in sanctification.

This side of heaven, we still struggle daily with sin. We are not perfect, but Paul talks about persevering until the day we are made perfect in heaven. I love that he doesn't just talk about sanctification, but he explains our motivation and how we are equipped – "because Christ Jesus has made me His own" (1 John 4:19; 1 Peter 1:5). In sanctification, God's grace continues to encompass us. He doesn't leave us on our own and say, "Go for it! See you at the finish line." We are His, and He is with us every step of the way.

Paul knows he isn't there yet. I think that shows his humility. All too often I fall into thinking I've arrived when I am far from it. However, Paul doesn't despair at not having reached the finish line. He perseveres. How does he do it? Paul says there is one thing he does: "forgetting what lies behind and straining forward to what lies ahead." Paul forgets the past, so he does not become content or complacent where he is. Each day is a new day to move forward.

Forgetting the past also means it doesn't have a negative hold on or influence over us. We can remember what God has done in the past and let that encourage us for today, but we don't camp there. In a race, you don't want to look behind and be distracted with who or what is behind you. If you aren't looking forward, you can run off course or crash into something. You are focused on what is before you – the finish line. Hebrews 12:1-2 repeats this idea. There we are throwing off the sin that hinders us, and our eyes are fixed on Jesus, the founder and perfecter of our faith – a wonderful picture of sanctification.

As Paul is forgetting what lies behind, he is also straining forward to what lies ahead – the goal. The word for straining is another athletic term depicting someone in a race. Have you seen a close race right near the end? The athletes lean forward with their torso to push across the finish line first. The Greek also means "bearing towards a point." Paul is focused on the goal, the upward call of God in Christ, and he is giving his all to get there.

Our upward call is eternal life, and it comes from God (Romans 6:23). Christ is our only means to get there. Yes, God gives us our part in obedience, but that obedience is only possible because of Christ's perfect obedience. His death and resurrection freed us from the power of sin; freed us from the old man, so that we can press onward.

For Reflection: What is an area in your walk with God that you have become complacent in? Somebody once told me that the way their marriage was worked for them. That stuck with me because I know I can get into that same kind of thinking. It isn't about what works for me but what God calls me to. When you think of what you have become complacent about, look to God's Word for what the goal is regarding it. We won't fully attain the goal here on earth, but Jesus has. In Him, we can keep straining forward.

Day 25 ~ Philippians 3:15-16

Let those of us who are mature think this way, and if in anything you think otherwise, God will reveal that also to you. Only let us hold true to what we have attained.

Yesterday we looked at Paul's pursuit of the goal (eternity in heaven where he would truly be perfect) and the one thing he did to get there. Today he calls us to the same pursuit. The word mature is the same word translated perfect in verse 12. Just as Paul said he had not yet reached spiritual perfection, he is calling those who are on the sanctification path – not perfect but pursuing God. He calls them to have the same thinking about their sanctification that he does. Forget what is behind and press onward towards Christ and eternal glory.

Paul realized that some might have different thinking. Maybe they saw something other than knowing Christ as most important, but Paul had confidence that God could show them what they needed to see. Paul presented truth, but understood it was up to God to open eyes and change hearts.

The phrase "hold true" conjures up the image of soldiers marching in a row. There is a direction and a purpose. We are to keep going in what we have attained. In Christ, we have His righteousness, we are free from the power of sin, and we are pressing on towards heaven (verses 9-14). Sounds simple, but we know from Romans 7:15-25 that Paul battled with doing the good he wanted to and keeping from doing the evil he did not want to do. In verse 18, he says that nothing good dwells in him (his flesh) and that he does not have the ability to carry out the right desires he has. He ends chapter 7 with thanks to God because in Christ is the only way we can keep going in what glorifies God.

Paul is again encouraging unity especially by using the phrase "let us." This is something that the Philippians knew they were to obey (2:1-2). Legalists wanted to divide. The Philippians faced pressure from outside sources (1:27-30) and from those within the church (3:2). Paul wanted them to be unified, not divided, under pressure.

For Reflection: Do you have questions about your sanctification? Doctrines you aren't sure about? Pray and ask God for wisdom and seek out someone spiritually mature to help you study God's word and understand. This is part of how we grow.

What things do you know, but are not walking in obedience to? What steps can you take to get back on track? Start with repentance and basking in God's grace and forgiveness.

Day 26 ~ Philippians 3:17-21

Brothers, join in imitating me, and keep your eyes on those who walk according to the example you have in us. For many, of whom I have often told you and now tell you even with tears, walk as enemies of the cross of Christ. Their end is destruction, their god is their belly, and they glory in their shame, with minds set on earthly things. But our citizenship is in heaven, and from it we await a Savior, the Lord Jesus Christ, who will transform our lowly body to be like His glorious body, by the power that enables Him even to subject all things to Himself.

There are two men and their wives that come immediately to mind when I think of spiritual mentors. One was the pastor and his wife at my church in California. The other was an associate pastor and his wife at the same church. They were grounded in Scripture, but could teach it in a way that resonated, convicted and encouraged. As much as I thrived on the teaching, it was their lives that made lasting impact. They were humble. They were not afraid or embarrassed to show where they struggled in their walks. They were real. They were servants. They never made me feel as if they were on a Super Christian pedestal above me. It felt like the four of them walked side by side with me. Brothers and sisters in Christ like these are treasured gifts.

We are biting off a bigger chunk today. At first I was going to skip verse 17, but as I read through chapter 3 today, verse 17 jumped out at me. In some ways it is a summary of Paul's instructions in chapters 2 and 3. He's given examples of Jesus, himself, Timothy and Epaphroditus. He now calls the Philippians to join with him in following godly examples. This is discipleship. The spiritually mature help others grow to be more Christlike by their life and teaching. God created us to help each other on this journey of sanctification (Titus 2:1-8). Paul's words in 1:27 exemplify this, "striving side by side". This is what will enable us not to be like those in verses 18-19.

I've read several different ideas on who these enemies are in 3:18. They could have been the Judaizers, ones who professed Christ or those who thought of Christ as only a spirit and therefore unable to bring salvation through a physical body. Regardless of who they were, we know that Paul was grieved because they were enemies of the cross of Christ – the gospel. The Greek word for enemy describes one who opposes God in their mind or one who is hostile. They either added to Christ's atoning work on the cross as if His death were insufficient or lived as if His sacrifice didn't matter.

In 3:19, Paul tells us that these enemies are doomed for hell (Romans 6:21) because their focus on self (contrast with 2:3-8) and on earthly things instead of on Christ. "Their god is their belly" means they sin through gluttony. They care only about their sensual appetites. This can be done by enforcing man-made dietary restrictions or by over indulging. They also glory in their shame. They didn't just sin, but instead of being repentant, they would boast of their sin. Their final description is that they set their minds on earthly things. In 3:12-14 Paul said he strived towards Christ and glory. These enemies are striving after and putting their confidence in earthly things not in Christ.

This is not who we are! We are citizens of heaven. We wait for Christ's return when He will transform us in glory to be like Him. As citizens of heaven, our words and actions should line up with those of our Lord. Our mission should be the same as God's. In Colossians 3:1-4 Paul says to set our minds on things above not on the things of this earth. We are different. Our focus is on God and the things of God. As we look to and study the things of God, our citizenship will be evident.

Some of the Thessalonians took this to an extreme. They were so focused on Christ's return, that they quit working and became a burden to others around them as they couldn't support themselves (2 Thessalonians 3:6-15). This is not Paul's intent. We can glorify God wherever He has called you whether in ministry, a job or our families.

Paul encourages us with two things. First, Christ's power will enable Him to subject all things to Himself. What a comfort to know that Christ has all power and that His power is working for us. By His power we will be transformed. Second, as Paul commands the Philippians to stand firm, he expresses his great love for them by calling them his "brothers" and his "joy and crown" (4:1). There is no doubting how much Paul loves and values his Philippian brothers and sisters.

For Reflection: Does your life reflect your citizenship? If not, what areas need to change?

In Titus 2:1-8, we see the pattern for discipleship. Do you have someone to mentor you? Are you mentoring someone? If your answers are no, pray about who God would have you strive side by side with.

Day 27 ~ Philippians 4:1-5

Therefore, my brothers, whom I love and long for, my joy and crown, stand firm thus in the Lord my beloved. I entreat Euodia and I entreat Syntyche to agree in the Lord. Yes, I ask you also, true companion, help these women, who have labored side by side with me in the gospel together with Clement and the rest of my fellow works, whose names are in the book of life. Rejoice in the Lord always; again I will say, rejoice. Let your reasonableness be known by everyone. The Lord is at hand.

On a mission trip to Honduras, we were painting classrooms at a seminary. At home, I don't think twice about getting good semi-gloss paint and doing as many coats as I need, but in Honduras, it is different. There aren't always the resources for the best paint. Often paint is watered down to stretch it, and if one coat gets some color up, one coat is ok. The man in charge of maintenance wanted to water down the paint like would normally be done. As our team was able to buy the paint, I wanted to make sure we did good coverage. But more importantly I didn't want to cause a rift with this man who we were trying to partner with or cause trouble between our missionary friends who lived in Honduras and the staff at the seminary. I am thankful that we all were willing to adjust to avoid conflict, and that God resolved it. The maintenance man has become one of our dearest brothers in Christ. It is inevitable that conflicts will come up in the church, but we have a choice how we handle them.

Paul is about to address conflict in the church. His entreaty to the two women in conflict and the "true companion" who can help encourage reconciliation is easier to receive when it is in the context of love (verse 1). Whenever confronting or correcting someone, we should always do it in love (Ephesians 4:15), which might require pausing, praying and checking our own heart first.

Note that Paul's direction to the two women is brief. He asks the true companion who is there in person to be the one to help the women reconcile. God's design for the local church body is to help each other and bear one another's burdens (Galatians 6:2). In verse 3, Paul affirms the value of these two women as co-laborers. The goal when there is conflict in the church is not only reconciliation but their restoration to their part in the ministry of the body.

We don't know what the conflict was between Euodia and Syntyche (verse 2). Those Paul was writing to would have known what it was. For us, it is beneficial that it is unknown because what Paul teaches in 4:4-9 is applicable to many conflicts. Much of our conflict comes from not getting what we want or think we deserve. We are discontent with the person or situation, and ultimately, we are discontent with how God has designed that circumstance in our life.

Paul's solution? The first part is to rejoice in the Lord always. And then he repeats it. Have you ever given a child an instruction, they don't obey, and you have to repeat, often multiple times? Joy is something we need to be reminded of again and again. It does not come naturally to us, and we tend to default to grumbling and questioning (2:14). But Paul says to rejoice! He also says to do it always. In the midst of a conflict, it's difficult to see reasons to rejoice, much less to be always rejoicing! The key is that Paul says to "rejoice *in the Lord* always." In chapters 1 and 2, Paul gave us many reasons in Christ of why we can always rejoice no matter what our circumstances. Christ paying for our sin, imputing His righteousness to us, victory over sin and death, and eternal life with Him are more than enough reasons to always rejoice. Those are just the tip of the iceberg. In the song *10,000 Reasons* Matt Redman sings there are "10,000 reasons for my heart to find" and I would venture to say there are even more if we kept on counting. [7]

A few years ago, I read through *One Thousand Gifts* Devotional: Reflections on Finding Everyday Graces by Ann Voskamp.[8] I was challenged to start writing down one thousand things I am thankful for especially in the everyday ways that God shows His grace. I began seeing how my day is full of things to be thankful for – from a hot shower to technology that allows me to communicate with family and friends around the world. Last year when our things were stolen in Honduras, our team sat down and began to think of all the things we had to be thankful for including our safety, that we had our passports and the way God provided the things we needed while we in Honduras. There are things all around just begging for us to really look, see God's grace and rejoice!

Paul's second step in resolving conflict is to let our reasonableness be known by everyone. The Greek word for reasonableness means "equitable, gentleness, moderation, being satisfied with less than one's due or the willingness not to retaliate" (2:1-5). Someone who is reasonable tries to see the other person's perspective. They are willing to overlook things in love if it is not a serious sin issue. They will let God fight the battle instead of fighting themselves. A reasonable person will patiently bear in affliction. Edward Welch writes, "Patience is interested in what direction people face. Do they face toward Jesus? Patience is more interested in direction and less interested in how fast people are changing."[9] Often others become more reasonable when we are reasonable towards them.

Paul finishes with "The Lord is at hand." It is reminder that Jesus is returning both at the rapture to take believers to heaven for eternal life with Him and in judgment to settle all the wrongs. Everyone will give an account to

Him. We want to do everything we can to be at peace with others (Romans 12:18).

For Reflection: Is there someone you need to reconcile with? What action can you take to pursue peace with them?

Do you choose joy? If you are not characterized by joyfulness, start by daily writing down things you are thankful for. Start with things Christ has done for you. Then begin to include everyday things like washing clothes (having clothes to wash, water to wash with, etc.).

Day 28 ~ Philippians 4:6-7

Do not be anxious about anything, but in everything by prayer and supplication with thanksgiving let your requests be made known to God. And the peace of God, which surpasses all understanding, will guard your hearts and your minds in Christ Jesus.

Have you ever prayed for peace? I have, but as I began to study these verses several years ago, I shifted some of my thinking. I realized that there are things that precede the peace of God guarding our hearts and minds. To review our context, this chapter began with a conflict between two women. Paul's first steps towards reconciliation (that we saw yesterday) were to rejoice and then let your reasonableness be evident. Here he gives us the next steps.

First, do not be anxious. The Greek *merimnaō* means "to be troubled with cares, worry, to seek to promote one's interests." The root word in Old English meant to strangle. Although we don't know what Euodia and Syntyche were disagreeing over, in the solution Paul addresses worry. If we think of some of our own disagreements, we can probably see worry woven through it. Worry that our opinions aren't being heard or valued. Worried that a need (real or otherwise) isn't being met. Worried what others will think of us. The list goes on. Looking at the Greek meaning we see that worry is often, if not always, about promoting our own interests.

The Greek also connotes the idea of an unnecessary or unfounded worry. If we stop and think about what we are worried about and then meditate on God's character, I think we will find that the worry fades away. God is omniscient, which means He knows all about the situation. He knows it fully where we know only our own perspective. He has all wisdom, so He knows best how to handle the situation. He is omnipotent, so there is nothing that can prevent Him from taking care of the situation. He loves us and always has our best in mind. You get the idea.

We have likely all heard of various tests showing the effects worry can have on our physical health. Because worry does not trust God, it affects us spiritually. Worry affects every part of us. The antidote is prayer.

Paul says not to worry about anything, but in everything present your requests to God. There is nothing that is left outside of prayer. Take everything to God and do it with thanksgiving. We can be thankful as we think of God's character and that He is all-sufficient to handle anything. The more I take my worries to God in the context of His character, my worries often become smaller in light of the grandeur of God.

I pray regularly for our Youth Group kids. If you have ever been around a teenager, you know there are many things to worry about. I remind myself that God is sovereign. He is in control of the situation in the kid's life even if it seems out of control to me. He loves that kid more than I do. He is good and is working what is best in their life for their sanctification and His glory. He is faithful. He isn't going to forsake His child. Praying in this way helps me to look at what I'm worried about in a different way. The situation is still a concern, but I can pray with hope and thanksgiving for who God is, what He has done, and what He is capable of doing.

Paul follows with, "the peace of God which surpasses all understanding will guard our hearts and minds." He doesn't just say that God's peace will come to us when we are wallowing in our sinful worry. Peace comes as we surrender our worry to Him with thanksgiving. God's peace isn't just a feeling.

Remember the conflict we began with. As we follow Paul's instructions, we can have peace with others because our whole perspective has changed.

This peace from God guards our hearts and minds. It helps to keep us from sinning in our situation. It keeps us from being strangled by the situation. It keeps us focused on Christ.

For Reflection: What are you worried about? Write down different attributes of God and how they apply to your worry. Then take it all to God with thanksgiving.

Day 29 ~ Philippians 4:8-9

Finally, brothers, whatever is true, whatever is honorable, whatever is just, whatever is pure, whatever is lovely, whatever is commendable, if there is any excellence, if there is anything worthy of praise, think about these things. What you have learned and heard and seen in me — practice these things, and the God of all peace will be with you.

I know that when I am in the midst of a conflict, my thoughts gravitate towards all the negatives about the situation or person, especially the person. I dwell on wrongs they've done in the past. I expect the worst response from them. I even conjure up how the conversation will go in my mind and it is never good. Positive aspects or points of thankfulness are harder to bring to mind. Paul's "finally" directs us to think on the excellent and good things. Not only is this crucial for conflicts, but it is beneficial as a pattern for our thought life throughout the day every day. This passage helps us counter our fears with truth.

Before we look at each specific component of our thinking, there are a couple general items. First, Paul uses "whatever" before each specific component. Whatever implies that the list is not exhaustive. There may be other aspects of thinking that fit into this God-centered mind set. Second, this list is not the whole or the end of the process. It is the preparation for Paul's command in verse 9 to put his teaching into practice. Right thinking will lead to right living.

Let's peer closer into Godly thinking which can only come out of our position of being in Christ who only, always had perfect, Godly thinking. True – God's Word is truth (John 17:17). We can focus on Scripture. Reading and memorizing Scripture are key to keeping our thinking Godly. Jesus is truth (John 14:6). We can think on the character and work of Christ, which will re-shape our thinking, words, and actions. In conflict, we can think on what is true about the person or situation based on the truth of Scripture. This might mean remembering that the other person is made in the image of God and loved by Him, that God is sovereign over the circumstance, or that our perspective is not the whole picture. When we struggle with fear of man, we can focus on the truth of who we are in Christ. It is God we are to please not man, and the Father sees us with Christ's righteousness.

Thinking on what is honorable is "to accord a great deal of respect due to wisdom, age, character, etc." This drives me to God's character first. Everything about Him deserves honor. In conflict, it helps dispel animosity when we think of honorable things in the other person. It is a rare occasion when there is not something we can find about the other person to honor. We know God has promised in His faithfulness that He will always give us a way out of temptation (1 Corinthians 10:13), so by the Spirit's work in us, we can choose what is honorable. We can have victory in Christ over lying, cheating or gossiping.

We know that God is just. When I meditate on God's justice, it is hard not to remember that when His justice demanded a penalty for sin, He executed that justice on His own Son so that He could shower mercy and grace on us. We can choose to respond with His grace and mercy to others because of the grace and mercy God showed us. We can see the things God says in Scripture about treating others fairly, not showing favoritism and defending the poor, the orphan and the widow. There are things we can do to advocate justice for them. Maybe it is by doing service projects for a widow or visiting them. We can volunteer, pray for or monetarily support orphanages and adoption. I love the variety of ways that Show Hope cares for orphans and promotes adoption. Maybe we help with a fundraiser for an alternative pregnancy center that supports young women through their pregnancy and after their baby is born. Jesus loved on the widows, oprhans and outcasts. Because of His redeeming work, we can too.

Pure means "chaste, modest, clean from every fault, exciting reverence." Again, my thinking goes to Jesus who was perfectly pure (1 John 3:3). Because He was clean from every fault, He was the only one who could atone for our sin. He imputes His purity or righteousness to us (1 Corinthians 1:30; 2 Corinthians 5:21) as well as to believers we are in conflict with. Through the Spirit, we can take our thoughts captive (2 Corinthians 10:5). We can choose to put restrictions on our computers and phones and seek accountability to combat pornography knowing that Jesus never looked lustfully at a woman. His record is ours.

Lovely is "what is pleasing." Eternity is not long enough to think on all that is pleasing about God. There is much in creation that is pleasing too. As my husband and I have traveled to different parts of the United States or to different countries, we see beauty in each one. Isaiah 53:2 describes Jesus this way, "He had no form or majesty that we should look at Him, and no beauty that we should desire Him." Jesus' outward appearance is not what made Him lovely. It was His character. We can also look for what is lovely in others. God made each of us unique and gave each of us gifts. We can express to them the things we find lovely about them for their edification.

Commendable means "marked by success, favorable or of good repute." Excellence is a "virtuous thought, feeling or action." Being worthy of praise means that something is worthy of commendation. We can see perfect pictures of each of these in God, and then we can look at God's imprints on others and situations. In 1 Corinthians 13:6, Paul in describing love says that it does not rejoice at wrongdoing but rejoices with the truth. When others do something commendable are we rejoicing with them or are we jealous and looking for things to criticize?

We are to think on these things. The Greek *loizomai* means, "to reckon inwardly, compute, calculate, dwell on, deliberate, meditate on." Paul is not calling us to a passing thought. He calls us to park on each one. How would we grow in our knowledge of God if we spent comprehensive time on each word in the list? How would our perspective of others or circumstances change if we dwelled on these Godly aspects rather than on negatives?

For Reflection: How and where has God grown you in this list of Godly thinking? Which areas do you need to grow more in? Write out specific things to think on for those areas.

Look again at verses 4-9. These verses contain both things we are to do and things that God does. In the space below, write out your responsibilities and God's promises.

My Responsibilties	God's Promises

Day 30 ~ Philippians 4:11-13

Not that I am speaking of being in need, for I have learned in whatever situation I am to be content. I know how to be brought low, and I know how to abound. In any and every circumstance, I have learned the secret of facing plenty and hunger, abundance and need. I can do all things through Him who strengthens me.

Verse 13 may be familiar to many of you. It is often quoted. People apply it to many things, but today let's look at it in context. We want to make sure we rightly handle the word of truth (2 Timothy 2:15).

Paul introduces this section in verse ten by rejoicing that the Philippian church had an opportunity to show their concern for Paul. We don't know if they didn't have resources or perhaps there was no way to get the resources to Paul. Whatever the reason the Philippian church had no opportunity, Paul is not rebuking them, or he would not have started verse ten with rejoicing. He has called them partners in the gospel (1:5) and in verses 14-18 he commends them for the gifts they have previously sent and the current one they sent through Epaphroditus.

Verse ten segues into Paul's exhortation on contentment. He is grateful for the Philippian's gift, but he has learned to be content whether he receives a gift or not. Paul compares several circumstances – good and bad. He had good times where his needs were met, and he found favor with people, but we also know he went through incredible hardships that most of us will never know. He repeats that "in any and every circumstance" he has learned how to face them, to be content.

Contentment does not come naturally to us. Grumbling and questioning do (2:14). When things are bad, we want better. More money. Bigger house. Well-behaved kids. Health. New car. Different job. But even when we have good things, we want more. There's always one more thing to have or change.

How did Paul do it? How did he have contentment in any and every circumstance? It was through Christ who gave him the strength. Throughout our study of Philippians, we have seen Paul point to Christ, desiring to know Him, and sacrificially serving Him. Paul's focus is not on himself or his needs. He knows that God is faithful and will supply every need we have (verse 19). We are also in Christ who was perfectly content in any and every circumstance. We will have days of grumbling and questioning, but on those days, Christ stands in our place with His perfect contentment.

So, when we read that Paul "can do all things through Him who strengthens me," we see that it is choosing contentment in and every circumstance. Does God equip us for the things He calls us to? Yes, we see that in other parts of Scripture, but here in verse 13, Paul's emphatic statement of doing all things is being content.

For Reflection: Where are you not choosing contentment? Confess that to God, and then write down the ways God has provided particularly in the situation you have been discontent. Be thankful that you can choose contentment in any and every situation because Christ's strength has equipped you.

Day 31 ~ Philippians 4:10, 14-18

I rejoiced in the Lord greatly that now at length you have revived your concern for me. You were indeed concerned for me, but you had no opportunity... Yet it was kind of you to share my trouble. And you Philippians yourselves know that in the beginning of the gospel, when I left Macedonia, no church entered into partnership with me in giving and receiving, except you only. Even in Thessalonica you sent me help for my needs once and again. Not that I seek the gift, but I seek the fruit that increases to your credit. I have received full payment, and more. I am well supplied, having received from Epaphroditus the gifts you sent, a fragrant offering, a sacrifice acceptable and pleasing to God.

Hopefully in this journey through Philippians, we have seen the many times Paul has moved us towards thanksgiving and joy in every circumstance. Here in chapter 4, Paul gets specific in thanksgiving to the Philippians and to God for the provision He supplied through the Philippians.

He describes their gifts in three ways: First, as a budding tree in verse 10. The Greek word translated as *revived* in the ESV is *anathallō* meaning to sprout or flourish again. The word *opportunity* is *kairos* referring more to a season not chronological time. The idea is that their gift bloomed in season. God knew when it was needed for the Philippians to be able to get a gift to Paul again. Paul never spiraled into panic mode or manipulated churches into giving. He trusted God's sovereignty and perfect timing.

Second, Paul says their gifts are an investment (verses 14-17). The Philippians gave material gifts to Paul and his ministry. Unlike the United States prison system, prisoners in Paul's time got food, clothing and any other needs from family and friends. It is still this way in some countries today. The return on their investment was spiritual through Paul's teaching and discipleship.

Third, Paul calls their gifts a "fragrant offering, a sacrifice acceptable and pleasing to God." We touched on this when we looked at Philippians 2:17-18 on Day 17. Their gifts were evidence of the fruit of their faith which brought glory to God. Their gift was a sacrifice because it was given out of their poverty not abundance (2 Corinthians 8:2).

In verse 14, Paul expresses gratitude that the Philippians shared in his trouble. Our English word *kind* might better be translated as excellent or honorable with no room for blame. *Thlipsis*, the Greek for "to share my trouble" carries the image of being pressed together, oppression and affliction. The Philippians were willing and did support Paul through severe trials. They did not shrink back when things got hard.

Finally, Paul in verse 16 esteems the Philippians for giving repeatedly. How often do we give once and think that is good enough? Are we continually seeking God for where He wants us to continue to give? Their repeated gifts were an encouragement to God. As my husband and I have led several mission trips to Honduras, it has been an encouragement to us not only that people have given to support the projects, but that many have given every time we have gone to Honduras. It has given us a sense we are part of a team with them even if they are not physically going with us each year.

For Reflection: Several years ago, a friend told me she had started praying over the checks she wrote to the church and for various missionaries and ministries, that God would use them for His glory. It challenged me to reflect on our giving – to be thankful that God has provided for us that we might give back and to be prayerful that God would use our gifts as an encouragement to those in ministry and for His glory.

Consider your own giving. Are you giving? Do you give only out of your abundance or do you give sacrificially? Are you checking off each month what you know you should do or giving out of thankfulness for what God has done and is doing? Are you seeking God for how He would have you keep giving or set on your current giving commitments?

Day 32 ~ Philippians 4:19-20

And my God will supply every need of yours according to His riches in glory in Christ Jesus. To our God and Father be glory forever and ever. Amen.

Let's look at some of the last truths Paul shares with us in this letter. Yesterday Paul challenged us with being content in any and every circumstance. Today he directs us towards God's faithfulness and provision, "And my God will supply every need of yours according to His riches in glory in Christ Jesus."

Have you every heard a child plead, "But Mom, I *neeeeed* this toy!" Or iPod, phone, outfit, money to go out with friends, or, or, or. As adults we usually look at those pleas and dismiss them. We know that kids don't really need those things. How often as adults do we do the same thing in our minds or before God? We each have our little (or big) lists of things we think we need.

1 Timothy 6:6-8 tells us, "Now there is great gain in godliness with contentment, for we brought nothing into the world, and we cannot take anything out of the world. But if we have food and clothing, with these we will be content." Paul, what about my bigger house? A car? A new couch? The list of needs Paul gives us is pretty short. He doesn't even have a good job on the list.

Are food and clothing our only needs? Flip back to chapter 3. Paul declared that everything was rubbish compared to knowing Christ. Our greatest need is Christ. If we have faith in Christ, God in His grace meets our greatest need (Ephesians 2:8-9). God is never stingy. He also gave us His Spirit to indwell believers. The Spirit is our Helper, Comforter, the One who convicts and the One who helps us understand God's Word. God has given us His Word, which is everything we need for life and godliness (2 Peter 1:3). He freed us from condemnation (Romans 8:1). He granted us forgiveness, Christ's righteousness and eternal life. He made us His children and heirs (Romans 8:12-17). I could keep going, but suffice it to say, God has lavished us with spiritual blessings to meet our needs. And I daresay that if we but pause, we will see that He has given us more than just clothing and food.

God is generous. Notice that God's supply is "according to His riches" not "out of His riches." What is the difference? Giving out of one's wealth could be any amount. You might have a million dollars, but you give ten. Giving according to one's wealth means that the amount given is in line with the wealth. We know that all things belong to God. He has immeasurable wealth. His gifts reflect His unlimited resources.

What is the fitting response to God's abundant supply of our needs? Contentment, yes, but praise as well. He is to receive our praise and thanksgiving forever and ever. We recognize that everything we have is a good gift from Him.

For Reflection: Praise God for His abundant provision. Write out ways that He has provided for your needs and beyond. Include both material and spiritual provisions.

Day 33 ~ Philippians 4:21-23

Greet every saint in Christ Jesus. The brothers who are with me greet you. All the saints greet you, especially those of Caesar's household. The grace of the Lord Jesus Christ be with your spirit.

We made it to our last day of journeying into Philippians together! Paul typically wraps up his letters with specific greetings. These verses are an encouragement to fellowship with other believers, to recognize the blessing of the family of God. I think of a typical Sunday morning and the people I greet. I realize there isn't time on a given Sunday to greet all the people in your local church unless it is very small, but this does challenge me to be more purposeful in getting out of my comfort zone and greeting more than those I am closest too. It may mean connecting with people during the week whether calling them or connecting in small groups or other ways.

Paul sends greetings from those that are with him "especially those of Caesar's household." Easy to read over that, but there is ginormous praise in there. Luke 15 contains several parables about the joy in lost things being found. Caesar referred to himself as a god. He persecuted Christians. That some in Caesar's household - those in his direct employ, Paul's guards – had come to saving faith was a point of rejoicing. The lost had been found and right there in the household of someone directly opposed to God.

Paul ends as he began – with grace. We need God's grace in salvation, but we also are dependent on it every day. We can only live a life glorifying to

God by His grace. It will never be by our own efforts. It is the grace of the Lord Jesus Christ. Paul has referred to Christ forty times in this short letter. He reminds us repeatedly Who is central to our lives.

For Reflection: Who can you make a point of fellowshipping with this week who might not be on your regular weekly radar? Who can you rejoice over that God has brought them to saving faith?

Do you think daily of your need for God's grace? Where specifically do you need to depend on Him today?

Songs for Philippians

I have tried to put the original information for each song. You may have a particular artist and version that you like best. I do!

Wesley, Charles. "And Can It Be." 1738.

Byrne, Mary E. "Be Thou My Vision." 1905.

Nockels, Christy. "Everything Is Mine In You." Let It Be Jesus. 2015.

Getty, Keith and Kristyn. "For The Cause." Facing A Task Unfinished. 2016.

Moen, Don. "Give Thanks With A Grateful Heart." Give Thanks. 1995.

Nordeman, Nichole. "Gratitude." Woven & Spun. 2002.

Paris, Twila. "He Is Exalted." Kingdom Seekers. 1985.

Frey, Marvin. "He Is Lord." 1977.

Assad, Audrey. "Humble." Fortunate Fall. 2013

Getty, Keith and Townsend, Stuart. "In Christ Alone." ThankYou Music. 2002.

Spafford, Horatio G. "It Is Well With My Soul." 1873.

Hearn, Naida. "Jesus Name Above All Names." 1974.

Getty, Keith and Kristyn. "Jesus, Draw Me Ever Nearer." In Christ Alone. 2006.

Kendrick, Graham. "Knowing You." Make Way Music. 1993.

Nockels, Christy. "Let It Be Jesus." Let It Be Jesus. 2015

Founds. Rick. "Lord, I Lift Your Name on High." 1989.

Bourue, Jeff. "Never Cease to Praise." Cumberland Belle Music. 2004.

Third Day. "Nothing Compares." Come Together. 2001.

Hawkins (Hwang), Katherine. "One Pure and Holy Passion." All My Heart. 2012.

Grotenhuis, Dale. "Rejoice In The Lord Always." 1985.

Sidewalk Prophets. "To Live Is Christ." Something Different. 2015.

Altrogge, Mark and Kauflin, Bob (Sovereign Grace Music). "To Live Is Christ." Risen. 2011.

Paris, Twila. "We Bow Down." The Warrior Is A Child. 1984.

Watts, Isaac. "When I Survey The Wondrous Cross." 1707.

Agnew, Todd. "Your Great Name." How To Be Loved. 2012

Endnotes

1. Bridges, Jerry, *Transforming Grace: Living Confidently in God's Unfailing Love* (Colorado Springs, CO: NavPress).

2. Erickson, Millard. *Christian Theology* (Grand Rapids, MI: Baker Books House), p.967.

3. Bridges, Jerry. *The Discipline of Grace: God's Role and Our Role in the Pursuit of Holiness.* (Colorado Springs, CO: NavPress).

4. Watermark. "More Thank You'll Ever Know." A Grateful People. 2006.

5. Piper, John. "Glorifying God…Period." Campus Outreach Staff Conference. Orlando, FL. 15 July 2013

6. Fitzpatrick, Elyse M. *Found In Him: The Joy of the Incarnation and Our Union With Christ.* (Wheaton, IL: Crossway, 2013).

7. Redman, Matt. "10,000 Reasons." 10,000 Reasons. 2011.

8. Voskamp, Ann. *One Thousand Gifts Devotional: Reflections on Finding Everyday Graces.* (Grand Rapids, MI: Zondervan).

9. Welch, Edward T. *Side By Side: Walking With Others in Wisdom and Love.* (Wheaton, IL: Crossway, 2015), p. 136.